The Art of Shurret™

Louise McCrady

Revised and illustrated by Lady McCrady

Seventh Edition 1997

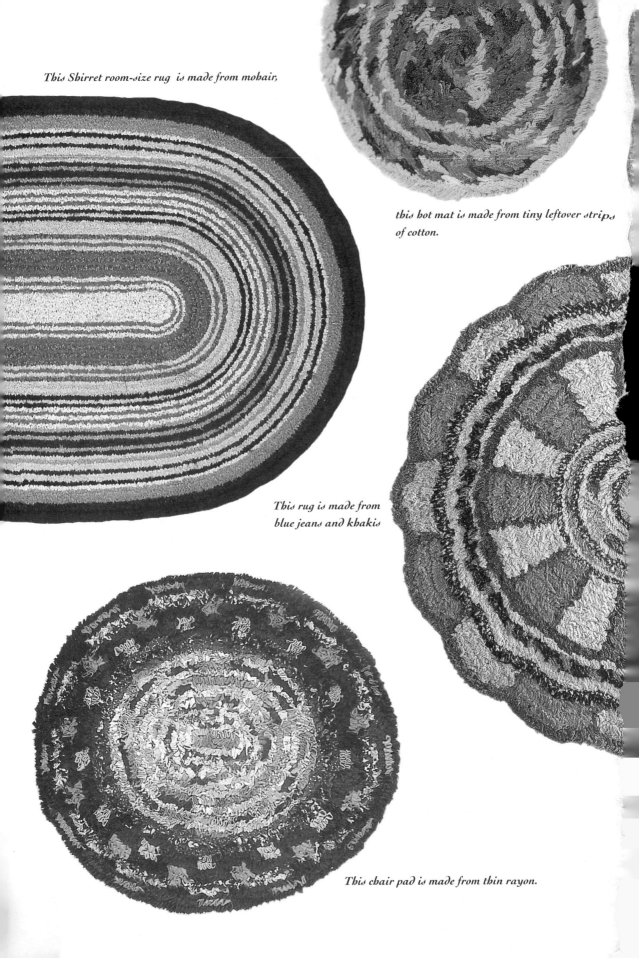

This Shirret room-size rug is made from mohair,

this hot mat is made from tiny leftover strips of cotton.

This rug is made from blue jeans and khakis

This chair pad is made from thin rayon.

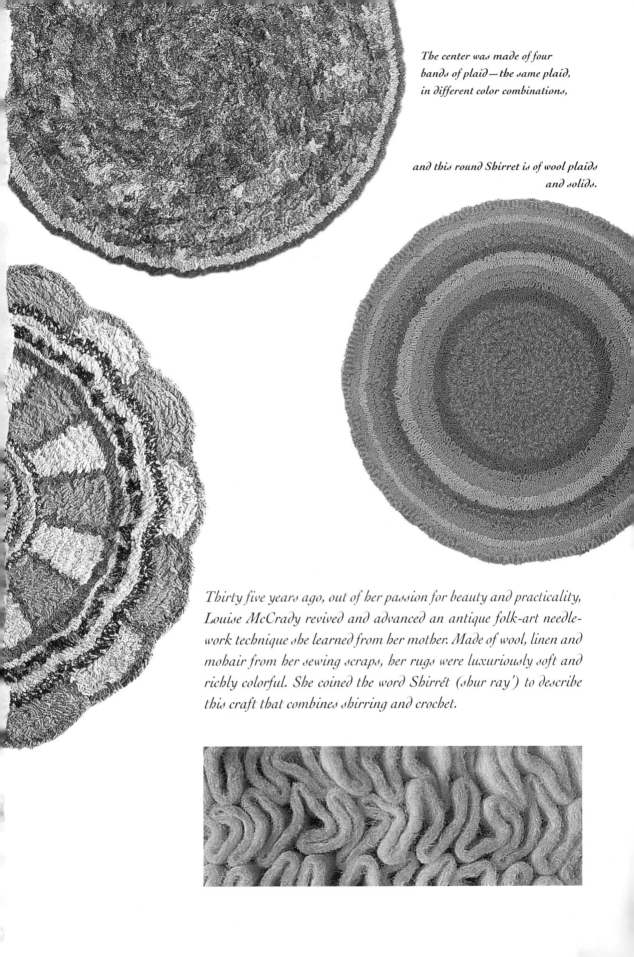

The center was made of four
bands of plaid—the same plaid,
in different color combinations,

and this round Shirret is of wool plaids
and solids.

Thirty five years ago, out of her passion for beauty and practicality,
Louise McCrady revived and advanced an antique folk-art needlework technique she learned from her mother. Made of wool, linen and
mohair from her sewing scraps, her rugs were luxuriously soft and
richly colorful. She coined the word Shirrét (shur ray') to describe
this craft that combines shirring and crochet.

Love to Harry & Bettina

Inquiries should be addressed to:

Shirrét America

P.O. Box 1338

Madison CT 06443 USA

International Standard Book Number: 0-9659579-4-2
Library of Congress Catalog Card Number: 97-92527
Manufactured in the United States of America

The Art of Shirrét

Copyright © 1997 Lady McCrady
Copyright © 1968, 1970, 1971, 1972, 1977 Louise McCrady.

Important Notice

All rights reserved. No part of this book may be reproduced or utilized in any form or by any means, electronic or mechanical, including photocopying, transmission, recording or by any information storage and retrieval system. All written instructions, illustrations, diagrams, and photos are copyrighted under U.S. and international copyright laws. Reproduction in any manner is prohibited. Neither single nor multiple copies may be made without written permission from the author.

This book is dedicated to my mother, Katherine Elizabeth Ent Benson, who was brilliant at problem-solving and extraordinarily good and kind. I loved listening to her stories…especially the ones about her mother, Addie Hart. As a little girl living in a small settlement where the Indiana State House now stands, she listened to wolves in the moonlight.

— Louise McCrady

This edition is dedicated to my mother, Louise "Toni Benson" McCrady, creative, charming, brainy and beautiful, the originator of Shirrét. She married the great nephew of "Blue Jeans" Williams, member of Congress and beloved governor of Indiana who, I've just discovered, had the State House built.

—Lady McCrady

The Origins of Shirrét

Thirty five years ago, out of her passion for beauty and practicality, my mother, Louise McCrady, perfected and advanced a basic folk art rugmaking technique she learned as a girl from her mother into an American needlework movement called Shirrét. She coined the word to describe the set of steps that begin with the unusual combination of shirring and crochet.

Katherine Benson, her mother, my grandmother—taught women in the Midwest to make rag rugs from the cotton polka-dot and cabbage-rose-print sewing scraps of their dresses. Using her mother's basic techniques, Louise developed new, repeatable methods that gave reliable results, and in so doing created the beautiful needlework technique that is known as Shirrét.

Whenever she demonstrated Shirrét at craft and country fairs, as she did 25 weekends a year for 25 years, people were intrigued by this new form of American rugmaking. These beautiful rugs, which begin as old clothes, look like museum-quality antiques that have been restored to rich colors! People love the surprise of fabrics that transform into totally different patterns by the process of Shirrét.

Shirrét is now in the third generation of our family. To mark its 30th anniversary, I have revised and added new illustrations to *The Art of Shirrét* for the publication of this seventh edition. With this book, the basic equipment, and your recycled clothing and fabrics, you'll have the makings for many delightfully creative and satisfying projects that will express your own personality. You can enjoy your Shirrét for years to come—and then pass it on for future generations to learn and enjoy.

Over the past few decades, enthusiastic Shirréters have taught hundreds of classes and made thousands of prize-winning Shirrét rugs and chair pads. "The Shirrét Lady" always encouraged Shirrét friends to send photos of their rugs to her, and to telephone "any time, day or night."

When I look at Louise's Shirrét rugs, they are filled with the beautiful clothes she tailored for us, and with her stories about my grandmother and great aunts. She had such fun doing Shirrét! A few hours of quiet Shirréting also gave my mother new perceptions and clear solutions to problems and questions. Louise's vitality, charm and enormous energy have been an inspiration to everyone she worked with—needleworkers, crafts people, teachers, librarians, editors, musicians and artists. All our love to you, Louise.

—Lady McCrady

Louise McCrady, 1976

© All Copying Prohibited By Law

Table of Contents

© All Copying Prohibited By Law

Chapter Three

Making Shirrét

Chapter Four

Using Shirrét

Patterns

© All Copying Prohibited By Law

© All Copying Prohibited By Law

Preface

VIDEOS!

What's the **Secret** to Shirrét™? The unique needle. It bastes. It crochets. It fits gently between your fingers.

What's the Secret for super fast stitching? Hold it just like I show you. Use my exact tension.

america shirrets .com now ! *Ta Dah !*

© All Copying Prohibited By Law

A letter from Louise McCrady

—Reprinted from the original edition

Welcome to the exciting and unique needlecraft called Shirrét. Shirrét will bring you years of pleasure, not only from learning and pursuing the craft itself, but also from the lasting beauty of the many rugs, chair pads, patchwork samplers and hearth rugs you will make.

I've included *everything you could ever want to know* about Shirrét in this book; yet the Shirret technique is simple, fun and easy, as you'll see.

Even I, after thousands of hours doing Shirrét, still find my fingers are a little clumsy manipulating the first starting rows of a new piece. But this passes quickly once you are past the first rows. So please don't give up in the beginning. With a little practice you will be Shirréting like an expert and loving every minute of it! And you will have a fascinating needlecraft to enjoy for many, many years. Hooray for Shirrét!

© All Copying Prohibited By Law

Introduction

© All Copying Prohibited By Law

Shirrét is a new concept, and a new craft, for almost everyone. With a special needle and strong cord, you create a net of crochet stitches that hold together the fabric zig zags called "folds." As you crochet with the cord using the special needle, you build thickness by adding a fold of fabric from the needle to each crochet stitch.

Shirrét is really a very easy technique. But remember, learning any new skill does require patience in the beginning. If you follow the lessons step-by-step, you will be surprised to discover how quickly it will all fall into place.

Learning Shirrét is like learning to ride a bicycle. It takes patience and concentration at first, and you may feel like giving up. You may feel ungrounded and out of control. Even experienced crocheters aren't accustomed to placing the Shirrét needle in between their middle and ring fingers, and it feels different to grasp the fingerhold with the middle finger. But holding the Shirrét needle correctly leaves fingers free to pull folds off the needle. Practice, have patience, and soon you'll be Shirréting! When you've got the rhythm, Shirrét is so relaxing. And think of the brain wave patterns it's creating!

If you are a crocheter, if a friend is teaching you, or if you can follow pictures or words, you're probably a natural Shirréter. First read the book from start to finish to pick up every detail, then practice to get the rhythm in your hands. This book will continue to be a reference tool, so keep it handy.

I suggust that you start with a sampler and move on to the table mat. The sampler is a little rug in miniature—the perfect size on which to practice and refine your skill. The method of starting is the same, whether the project is small or large. The sampler is designed to give you a worthwhile learning experience while acquiring understanding and experience. It's a good way to try different fabrics, color combinations and design ideas.

Thousands of people have learned to Shirrét from prior editions of *The Art of Shirrét.* You will, too, if you follow the lessons in this book, in order, without skipping any!

© All Copying Prohibited By Law

Chapter One
Planning Shirrét

This fabric   looks like this in Shirret!

Textural elements to design with

© All Copying Prohibited By Law

The way you use fabric in Shirrét is completely different from any other way you use fabric. In Shirrét you see the edges of the fabric, rather than the face. Thus, when you are filling the needle it doesn't matter if the fabric is wrong side out or right side out (except when you make the final round). Your authentic, if somewhat gaudy, muumuu from Hawaii is perfect for a Shirrét project, with its hot shades of chartreuse, even though the print is out of style!

A Shirrét can be a storehouse of memories of family events. One small rug might contain tiny baby corduroy overalls, Mom's hot pink linen scarf, husband's plaid flannel shirt from the Upper Peninsula, jeans from Paris and the Chanel jacket that got too tight in the arms. Decorators' fabric swatch books of medium weight, loosely woven linen-ey fabric (no chintz or tight polished cotton) offer a variety of color coordinated fabrics. Paint and wallpaper stores throw them out when they update every season.

Any shape that you can draw out on paper, such as the outline of a rabbit, can be made into Shirrét! You can draw pattern pieces to put together a Shirrét vest or slippers! Working in rows and rounds, you can also create geometric designs as you go, or chart them first and follow your pattern.

Thinking about color

Your Shirrét will become a wonderful splash of color and texture in your home, no matter where it's used—on the floor, on a table, on a chair. As you plan each project, think about where it will be used, and which colors might blend in the most pleasing, yet interesting, way.

Using complements on the color wheel—ultramarine blue with orange, violet with yellow, green with red, aqua with pink—lends brightness and richness to the colors. Pick colors with the same intensity or brightness and they'll almost pop as they grab your attention. Pale pink and turquoise wouldn't have as strong an effect as hot pink and turquoise. A pale geranium red combined with a willow green would have the same intensity; using color in this way makes a color look like more of itself.

You can use the combinations of the two color opposites to shade between them and gain a third color. For example, violet and yellow mixed together in paint make shades of gold, which would be a nice transition near or between the two colors. A clean cool blue and orange accentuate and enliven each other. In paint, a bit of red mixed with green would give a copperish color, whereas more green with a bit of red might be bronzey. The relationship of all four colors is interesting.

© All Copying Prohibited By Law

And don't forget to use the most subtle greys and neutrals to their advantage. Greys can come from patterned fabric as well as solid fabric, they can be warm (khaki, cream, pale mauve, pale olive) or cool (pale periwinkle, baby grey-blue, ice blue). Greys can give the eyes a rest and keep the color from being too intense, while paradoxically, making certain spots more intense.

These are techniques the French Impressionists discovered. Together, these colors create a hazy effect that dazzles in the way that Pierre Bonnard's paintings from the French Riviera did, or cheer you in the way of Mary Cassatt's portraits of mothers and children.

The occasional bright color was used in Amish interiors and quilts in relationship to workaday navy and black, which creates a gem-like quality.

Contemporary paintings offer color ideas. Mark Rothko's paintings vibrated in masses of yellows and golds (with a thin line of blue), or with fields of periwinkle blue and violet and a few spots of orange. Franz Kline chose equal amounts of black and white in energetic swashes to grab the eye. Susan Rothenberg limits her palette to two or three colors to create forceful images. Elizabeth Murray's paintings construct a riotously careful mix of fragmented color-forms. Joan Mitchell used colors from nature in relation to white and pale grays to express the effect of light on color.

As you progress, put your rug down on the floor often and view it from various positions. View the rug from the top of a flight of stairs or out the window to get perspective on the color relationships and how they blend or complement each other.

Look at your piece for its composition and balance. If it is a geometric, try to repeat as many of the fabrics as possible if it needs more balance. The fabric used for a center should be brought out in the body and repeated once or twice to avoid a "bulls-eye" effect. If you run out of the center fabric, substitute one that is similar in tone. If the color were turned into grey, would it be a light grey or a medium grey or a dark grey? Try to match the similarly colored fabric in this way.

If you aren't sure which color to add, cut a few strips and attach them to see what the effect is. Juxtapose speckled areas made with floral prints, plaids, stripes and checks with solid or heather areas for interest. You'll discover your style as you make more Shirrét. Color has meaning, and yours may be subtle, bold or in-between. Paintings identify artists, and your Shirrét will identify you.

Franz Kline, "Accent Grave"

What fabrics work, and why

Pure wool, or a blend of wool with other fibers, is the easiest and quickest fabric to work with and is an excellent choice for rugs and chair pads. It threads on the needle easily and works up faster than cotton because it has more body and bulk. It wears well, gives warmth, has rich color and texture, and resists soil. All weights and textures can be used and can be mixed in any given piece. In fact, a variety of weaves and textures adds interest to the work.

© All Copying Prohibited By Law

Thin dress-weight wool, firm-bodied flannel, loosely woven tweeds, and mohair can be combined to add textural interest. Bonded wool can be used as it is or, if bonding is loosely attached, it can be peeled off easily. Very firm, heavy wool, such as coating, is best reserved for the final finishing round.

Medium and loosely woven wool plaids and heathers merge and create a field of many colors packed closely together, even though they start out as folds.

Felt and firmer medium-weight wools (like the dyed solids used in rug hooking) always retain a zig-zag appearance in the rows and create visual interest.

Cotton, including blends of cotton with other fibers, is a good choice for table mats, practice pieces and kitchen and bathroom rugs, which will be washed frequently. The fabric should be sturdy with a fairly open weave so it can be threaded on the needle easily. Medium-weight duck, brushed denim, denim wrinkle cloth, butcher linen and sailcloth cotton are available in wonderful colors and prints. Cotton flannel and homespun have lovely, soft, velvety textures. Unbleached muslin can be dyed in desired shades or used for contrast with bright prints (and can be doubled for firmer body).

Corduroy is velvety to the touch. Velvet is soft, and velveteen is shimmery with rich color. Linen and rayon give a lacy effect.

Woven polyester, orlon, acrylics are easy to work with and soften on the cut edges to produce a velvety sheen.

Knits come in many forms: single knits, double knits, jersey knits, in cotton, wool, polyester, acrylic and nylon. Many work up nicely, while others, especially polyester double knits, are rather difficult to thread on the needle because of the thickness and impenetrability of the knit. You may want to sharpen the stopper end to a long tapering point to thread strips on and push them toward the hook end. Experiment with the knit fabric scraps you have to find which ones are easiest to work with. Use the rest for cleaning rags.

Where to find fabrics

Go through your closet. Look for outgrown and outmoded dresses, skirts, pants, jackets. Cut out the threadbare areas and discard. Explore your attic for old curtains, drapes, slipcovers, blankets, bedspreads, stained tablecloths, napkins, or dust ruffles. It doesn't matter if they are faded, as they will work up in soft pleasing tones and can still provide many years of good use, in a Shirrét.

- Dig up sewing scraps. Larger remnants can be used for background or color bands, smaller scraps for small pieces or potpourri areas.
- Ask your friends and neighbors to save their sewing scraps and old clothes and discards.
- Check out charity and thrift shops, Goodwill stores, rummage sales,

© All Copying Prohibited By Law

or garage sales—all very good sources for wool. You will find good quality fabrics in skirts, dresses, and jackets at bargain prices.

- Pore over remnant tables for misprints and irregulars. They can be used quite well.
- Visit mill-end stores and factory outlets, especially those that sell by the pound, for cuttings and bolt ends.
- Check the classified ads of needlecraft magazines.
- Salvage decorator, drapery and slipcover sample books from paint and decorator stores.

Fabrics to avoid (yet use if you must)

Some of you cringe at the idea of throwing anything away. Occasionally you have a quantity of fabric that isn't perfect for Shirrét but you just want to use it up. For example, some chintzes or heavy coating wools or polyester double knits are difficult to get onto the needle because they are too tightly woven.

You can still use them, if you remove the cap from the back end of the needle and sharpen the needle to a long tapering point. Thread strips on from the pointed end and push folds toward the hook end. You may find your stitchmaking is more tense when working with these fabrics, so try to keep stitches relaxed. If it is so tightly woven that the Shirrét stitch is difficult to make, choose an easier fabric. If a fabric is thin-bodied, consider it for small, delicate pieces. Thin, loose-weave wool or cotton or silk can be doubled by matching the cut ends and filling the needle starting from the doubled cut ends. Doubling helps the fabric to work up faster, and it provides visual interest.

Preparing the fabric

Loosely woven wool, woolish-polyester or loosely woven heavy-weight cotton is easiest to begin with. Don't use a wool *knit*. Use some ordinary fabric and some pieces with bright colors, and your first piece will look like folk art.

You can't put wool and cotton in the same piece, so pick one or the other. The rule for combining fabric is this: if they can be washed together, they can be in Shirrét together.

Look for old wool pants or a skirt, cut off the waistband and seam tape, undo the hem and press out the pleats, or find some wool fabric. Blue jeans, unless extremely soft, can be more difficult to pierce unless they've been soaked in fabric softener overnight.

© All Copying Prohibited By Law

Woven fabric is different from a fused fabric (like felt) or knitted fabric because you can see the crisscross of the weave. For Shirrét, woven fabrics are cut on the bias so they won't ravel or wear out. Strips can be any length, but are *always* 3/4" wide. Odd-shaped bits of fabric and whole pieces can easily be cut on the bias. Press fabric into folded pieces at the ironing board, and then move to a hard, flat surface for marking and cutting into strips.

Before cutting all your fabric into strips, try a few strips to make sure it can be easily threaded onto the Shirrét needle.

Used clothing: Prepare by cutting off collars, waistbands, zippers. Open hems, seams, and pleats so pieces lie flat.

Washing old fabrics: Put cut pieces of fabric in a mesh bag or pillow case to prevent unraveling in washer and dryer.

Wool: Flimsy or loosely woven wool can be improved by washing in very warm or hot water to shrink and tighten up the open weave.

Perma-Press: Crease-resistant fabrics have a resin finish that makes them firm-bodied. They will be softer and easier to thread on the needle if you add a strong solution of fabric softener to a pail of very hot water. Soak for hours or overnight. Spin and put in dryer with fabric softener sheets.

Old blue jeans: Treat like perma-press fabrics.

Non-colorfast fabrics: Soak 15 minutes in a solution of hot water and Borax to loosen excess dye. Rinse until water is clear.

Using the fabric

Before cutting all your fabric into strips, try a few strips first to be sure it is not too difficult to thread on the Shirrét needle. A good way to sample different weights and types of fabrics is to go through your sewing scraps. You will discover those you prefer working with and their various finished effects.

There are many blends of fibers, so if the fabrics look and feel compatible, they most likely will be. It is wise to refrain from knowingly combining 100% cotton with 100% wool because they will show wear differently with use, washing will be a problem, and they won't look right. *If a fabric looks like cotton, put it in a cotton piece. If it looks like wool, put it in a wool piece.*

© All Copying Prohibited By Law

How much fabric?

Approximately 1 yard of fabric makes a 12" x 12" square of Shirrét.

> *Wool*: 1 square foot of Shirrét - 12" x 12" - in rows, not rounds, uses 3/4 yard of 54"-60" medium weight wool or wool-acrylic blends.
> *Cotton*: 1 square foot of Shirrét - 12" x 12" - in rows, not rounds, uses 1 1/8 yard of 45" medium weight cotton and cotton-acrylic blends.

Round and oval pieces use more fabric because of the greater density in increase rounds.

You'll need more of thin fabric, less of thick fabric. (If fabric is thin, you can use it double thickness.)

What's in a scrap?

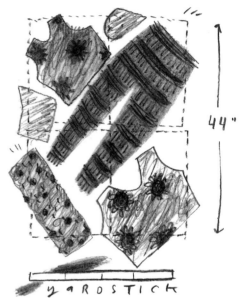

Lay your fabric scraps out across two open newspaper pages that you have measured to 45" or 54" or 60". You can determine how much yardage you have by measuring it with a yardstick in 1/4-yard lengths. If you have a yard, once you have cut all the pieces up you can separate it into four little plastic bags at 1/4 yard each. If you have 3/4 yard, split it into three bags of 1/4 yard each.

Estimating yardage

Put cut strips into individual bags with a note recording how much yardage is enclosed. It is helpful to divide a given amount of fabric into equal portions. Cut separately, and put into individual bags with notes: "1st 1/4 yard", "2nd 1/4 yard," "3rd and last 1/4 yard." When you have used the first bag of strips, you can count the number of rounds or rows made with that amount of fabric and estimate how many rows or rounds can be completed with the remaining bags of strips. Remember, as increases are added for round or oval pieces, more yardage will be required to complete each round.

© All Copying Prohibited By Law

Cutting bias strips

The easy Shirrét method you won't find anywhere else, and why you don't need a machine to cut alot, fast

To cut bias strips, follow these steps:

1. In new fabric and sewing scraps, lengthwise threads are parallel with selvedges. Crosswise threads go from selvedge to selvedge. Look closely and you can see the weave. Plaids and checks show the weave clearly.

    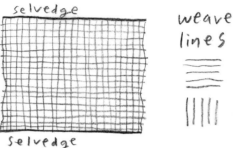

    If you have a yard of fabric cut it in four pieces. This will make it easier to cut through all the thicknesses of the fabric.

2. Lay a single thickness of 1/4 yard or less on the table in front of you. Turn it so the lines of the weave make an x.

    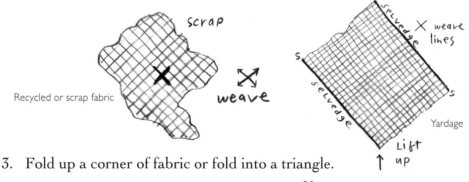

    Recycled or scrap fabric

3. Fold up a corner of fabric or fold into a triangle.

    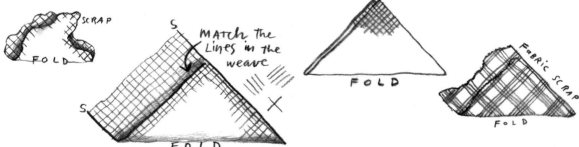

    With plaids or stripes, follow the pattern. With solid color or prints, line up threads by eye. Press fold.

© All Copying Prohibited By Law

4. Fold the folded edge over. Maximum height should be less than 8" or the length of the marking gauge. Line up weave lines and threads on all the edges. Press fold.

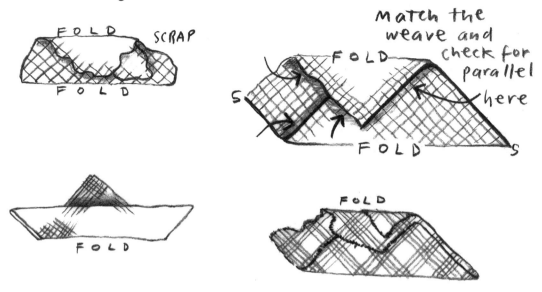

5. Continue folding fabric over until it is all folded into one long piece. Press.

6. Mark for cutting with 3/4" marking gauge and tailor's chalk or a sliver of soap. Mark across the narrow width like slices in a loaf of French bread. Begin marking at one end and mark across to other end. *Never use pencil. It will make cut edges look dirty.*

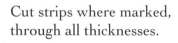

Cut strips where marked, through all thicknesses.

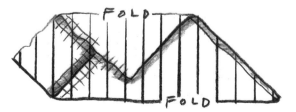

© All Copying Prohibited By Law

7. Square ends of strips by trimming off triangular ends.

Leftover bits for stuffing pillows.

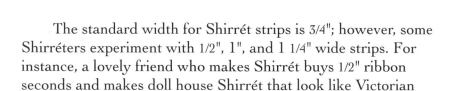

The standard width for Shirrét strips is 3/4"; however, some Shirréters experiment with 1/2", 1", and 1 1/4" wide strips. For instance, a lovely friend who makes Shirrét buys 1/2" ribbon seconds and makes doll house Shirrét that look like Victorian lace because the inner net of cord shows. A girlfriend in fashion uses loosely woven wool mohair cut to 1" wide strips to make fluffy Shirrét vests. (On a rug, the folds would fall over irregularly and disturb the design). And there is a gentleman who cuts up old coats of dense and thick fabric. His bias strips are 1 1/4" wide. Dense, heavy fabric is challenging to work with. In his rugs, the folds are more defined and the rugs are very sturdy and rich.

Doll house ribbon Shirrét

Helpful hints

> Fabric may be folded and pressed with either the right or wrong side out. Choose the side that will best show the lines drawn for cutting.

> If you fold the fabric into 8" widths, you won't have to shift the marking gauge each time you mark it and the marking and cutting will go quickly.

> Cut carefully, but a little unevenness won't be noticeable when worked into shirred folds. If the fabric slides or shifts, pin through center of marked strips before cutting.

© All Copying Prohibited By Law

Basic equipment

One of the great advantages of Shirrét is that it does not require expensive equipment and supplies.

Shirrét Needle. A specially designed needle with a long, slender shaft that permits easy penetration of fabric, and a hook on one end that is the correct size for making crochet stitches of cord. An important design feature is the fingerhold, which keeps the hook in the working position and prevents the needle from turning in the hand. Extra needles are not necessary, but are useful for changing colors and working faster (or in case you lose one!).

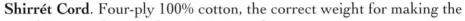

Shirrét Cord. Four-ply 100% cotton, the correct weight for making the Shirrét stitch, smooth to minimize splitting with the hook, strong to give the work great durability. Waxed linen is as strong as cotton, but it is 12 times the price of cotton cord. It is also possible that the wax might come off when Shirrét is washed and leave odd marks in the fabric.

Marking Gauge. A gauge of 3/4" x 8" for marking fabric to be cut into strips.

   © All Copying Prohibited By Law

Pin markers. Small safety pins without an extra coil at the end, which hang straight in the fold and do not twist or snag the fabric.

Slivers of soap. Save the very last flat bit you usually throw away for marking fabric strips for cutting. It makes a good, thin line! Collect slivers of different colors for marking dark and light fabrics. Tailor's chalk also works. It comes in assorted colors, and is available in a plastic case with chalk sharpener.

Scissors (or dressmaker shears). Must be sharp! Rotary cutter and cutting mat could also be used.

Believe it or not, cutting the strips with a rotary cutter or simple shears (rather than a cutting machine) has turned out to be the most quick and efficient way of cutting fabric for Shirrét.

Small clipping scissors.

Cord spindle. Holds the tube of cord and prevents tangling.

Note: Shirrét equipment—the book, needle, cord, marking gauge, and cord spindle—is available only by mail from Shirrét, P.O. Box 1338, Madison CT 06443. Send for color brochure and price list.

© All Copying Prohibited By Law

Chapter Two

Learning Shirrét

VIDEOS!

What's the **Secret** to Shirrét™?
The unique needle.
It bastes. It crochets.
It fits gently between your fingers.

What's the **Secret** *for super fast stitching?*
Hold it just like I show you. Use my exact tension.

america
shirrets
.com now !
Ta Dah !

© All Copying Prohibited By Law

Basic rules

There are five basic rules in Shirrét. They apply to all shapes: square, round or oval. You may want to learn and practice them while making the Shirrét Sampler (p. 39). Refer to these rules, and the glossary (p. 84) when you haven't done Shirrét for awhile to refresh your memory.

Rule #1: A Shirrét stitch consists of a crochet stitch of cord *plus* a shirred fold of fabric from the needle. There must be a fold of fabric after every stitch. While practicing say to yourself "First comes the stitch, next comes the fold." *A Shirrét stitch is not complete until a fold of fabric is added to the crochet stitch.*

Rule #2: Every row begins with 1½ folds. Look at the needle that you have filled with shirred folds. Notice that each individual strip of fabric can be flipped over on the needle. Turn the first strip over so the cut end near the hook is turning *away* from you. With left thumb and middle finger take hold of the folded edge of fabric on top of the needle: you are holding *one complete fold*. Next, turn the strip over so the cut end near the hook faces *toward* you. With left thumb and middle finger, take hold of this single thickness of fabric: you are holding *a half fold*. Now add the next complete fold that is on the needle: you are holding *1½ folds*. It is this 1½ folds that you will need in order to begin every new row.

Rule #3: Every row ends with 1½ folds. At the end of each row you will make 1 double crochet stitch between the last two folds and pull off one fold. To end the row, it is necessary to cut the strip of fabric. Slide your scissors through the center of the next fold still on the needle. On top of the needle, cut through the strip. The cut end of the strip will be facing you. Pull off this ½ fold, adding it to the last fold already pulled off. The row ends with 1½ folds. Remember: *when the cut end of a strip faces toward you, it is a half fold.*

Rule #4: There must be a "bridge" to each new row. Every row of a square or rectangle, and every round of an oval or a round, is a complete connected unit. To move up to the level of the new row or round, make two chain stitches of cord: this is the "bridge." Next, pull the first 1½ folds off the needle to start the new row.

Rule # 5: Always skip the first cord stitch of a new row. There are two strands of cord between all the shirred folds. These two strands of cord are called a "cord stitch." When starting a new row, skip the first cord stitch, which is between the first and second folds. Insert hook under both strands of the cord stitch between the second and third folds to make the first double crochet stitch of a new row. The only exception to this rule is when making *the first four rounds* of the center of a round piece.

Note: do not roll your Shirrét or leave it in a workbasket for long periods of time. It is better to lay the work flat between work periods, if possible.

© All Copying Prohibited By Law

Getting started—the "How To's" of successful Shirrét

The Shirrét needle is a specialized needle with a long slender shaft that permits easy penetration of fabric. The fingerhold keeps the hook in the working position and frees the thumb and forefinger for pushing off the folds.

You will need to practice to get used to holding the Shirrét needle correctly. Even though you may be an expert crocheter, you must learn a different way to hold this needle between your fingers to take advantage of the fingerhold. Practice the crochet stitches with just the cord at first to become familiar with the correct way to hold the needle. Also, this will help beginning crocheters learn the basic stitches and the correct way to control the tension of the cord.

If you revert to the way you hold a pencil or the way you always held a crochet needle, you won't be able to Shirrét with the folds of fabric.

Hold needle in a relaxed manner. It is not necessary to grip it tightly. The Shirrét needle is designed for ease in working. Your hand is in a natural, unbent position. Hand tension is reduced as long as you relax your grip on the needle.

How to hold the Shirrét needle

1. Place the needle on top of your right hand between your middle and ring fingers. The stopper end of the needle points toward your elbow. Pull the hook down over the front, perpendicular to your hand.

2. Now curl the middle finger around the fingerhold. Place thumb and forefinger near hook on the shank. Curl ring finger and pinky finger into palm of hand. Hook points downward.

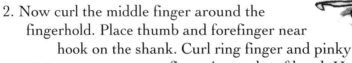

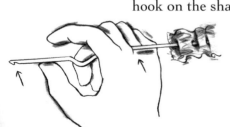

© All Copying Prohibited By Law

The needle feels most comfortable when it is filled with shirred folds. The shaft of the needle can also rest between the ring and pinky fingers. Use the position that is most natural and comfortable for you.

outside

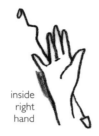

inside
right
hand

alternate position

Since left and right hands are equally active making Shirrét stitches, most left-handed people can work easily with the standard Shirrét needle, but a left-hand needle is available on request.

How to control the tension of the Shirrét cord

1. Bring cord inside palm of **left** hand.

2. Loop long end once around base of little finger and back to palm of hand.

3. Bring cord inside across little finger and next two fingers, then to outside of hand and back toward you over forefinger.

4. Keep forefinger extended and hold short end between thumb and middle finger. Curl other fingers into palm of hand. The left forefinger regulates the tension of the thread. Avoid making stitches over the top of the left forefinger.

© All Copying Prohibited By Law

5. The Shirrét cord should lie around fingers firmly enough to hold the tension, but not so tightly as to make it difficult to pull the loops through. Practice this so it becomes automatic, because the cord is constantly on the move through your fingers.

When the left hand works properly, the right hand can pull one crochet loop through another loop easily. The left hand pulls the thread slightly to the left, and the right hand pulls the needle slightly to the right.

How to make crochet stitches with the Shirrét needle and cord

Even if you are an expert crocheter, practice the crochet stitches with just the cord at first to become familiar with the correct way to hold the needle.

1. **Make slip loop in Shirrét cord.**
   To start, make a loop at end of cord by grasping cord about 6" from end. Lap long end over short end to form a loop. Hold between left thumb and forefinger. Push long end through first loop from back to front to form a second loop, and pull it out until knot tightens at base of loop. Insert hook in loop and pull long end of cord to regulate size of loop to approximately 1/4".

© All Copying Prohibited By Law

2. **Holding Shirrét needle in your hand correctly, make 16 chain stitches (ch st).** *Make chain stitches loose.*
   With a chain stitch, each loop is drawn through preceding loop. With starting slip loop on hook, pass hook under cord between forefinger and thumb, catch cord with hook and pull it through loop on hook to make 1 chain stitch.

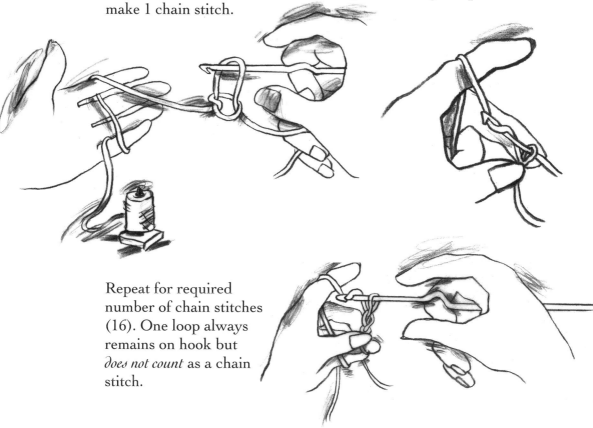

Repeat for required number of chain stitches (16). One loop always remains on hook but *does not count* as a chain stitch.

3. Turn. All rows will now be worked from right to left.

4. **Make a double crochet stitch (dc).**

   For the first row, put cord over hook. Insert hook under 2 top threads of fourth chain stitch from hook. Do not count loop on hook.

   Catch cord with hook and draw it through ch st (3 loops on needle).

© All Copying Prohibited By Law

Put cord over hook and draw it through two loops (2 loops left on needle).

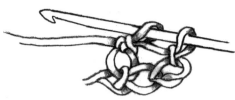

Again, put cord over hook and draw through last two loops (1 loop left on needle). 1 dc completed.

5. For next dc, put cord over, insert hook under 2 top threads of next ch st and proceed as before. Repeat across row (a total of 13 dc). At end of row, ch 3 and turn. End of row 1.

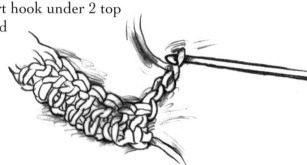

6. Second row. The ch 3 counts as first dc of new row. Put cord over and insert hook under 2 top threads of second st of previous row (5th ch from hook not including one on hook). Work dc to end of row (13 dc).

    Last dc of row is made in top of turning ch st of previous row.

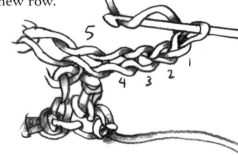

7. Continue for 7 rows. Fasten off. To fasten off, leave 4" and cut cord. Pull end through last loop on needle. Voila—c'est fini! Your crochet practice swatch is complete!

© All Copying Prohibited By Law

How to fill the Shirrét needle with shirred folds

Look for the longest strips of fabric you can find to simplify your stitch making in the first three rows. The cut strips of fabric are threaded onto the Shirrét needle to form the shirred folds.

Place entire right hand over the needle, with thumb and forefinger near hook. Do not be concerned about the position of the fingerhold or hook. Hold a strip of fabric in left hand between thumb and forefinger. Push hook down through center of strip about 1/4" from the cut end. Push the hook up into the center of the strip 3/8" - 1/2" from the first penetration. Pull on strip with left hand to make the fabric a little taut. Keep both hands close together.

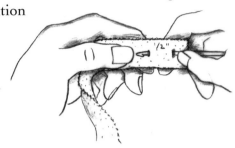

As this 1/2" space is pushed onto the needle, a fold is created.

Bring left hand back and forth across point so needle penetrates strip at even intervals. Keep right thumb on top of folds as you proceed. From time to time push folds back on shaft.

Continue to the end of strip, with last penetration about 1/4" from end. At end of the strip, if too much fabric remains, but not enough for an additional fold, trim off the excess beyond 1/4".

CUT excess BEYOND 1/4"

As you are filling the needle, do not be concerned about matching the right or wrong side of fabric.

Start another strip and use as many strips as are required to fill the needle to the fingerhold. When you have filled the needle past the fingerhold, it is full. You'll have room to make stitches with the space left. When you have filled the needle with shirred folds of fabric, you are ready to attach the folds to your work with crochet stitches of cord.

© All Copying Prohibited By Law

How to make continuous strips without sewing

In Shirrét, you never sew strips together. The tiniest strips can be used because the basic unit of fabric is a fold.

Making a continuous strip is easy. Always arrange the fabric on the needle as if it were connected. When the strip ends, start the next strip at the same place—facing up or facing down, above or below the needle—so the two ends would make a fold if they weren't cut.

When you Shirrét across a row you must be careful to pull off one *complete* fold after each stitch. This is easy because you can see the fold sitting on top of the needle. This is a fold.

FOLD

This is the same as a fold: Two cut ends facing the same way.

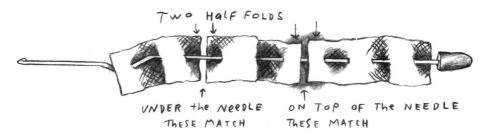

TWO HALF FOLDS

UNDER the NEeDLE THESE MATCH

ON TOP OF THE NEEDLE THESE MATCH

This is a half fold. If you come to a half fold and there isn't a half fold next to it on the needle, turn the whole strip over…

HALF FOLD

THESE DON'T MATCH

ROTATE the NEXT

STRIP on THE NEEDLE

… and you get another half fold to match it, to equal one fold.

Prepare to Shirrét with a filled needle by making sure each fold you will pull off is a full fold. Turn the strips over on the needle so the half folds face the same way.

You cannot make a dc if you've only pulled off a 1/2 fold. You need another 1/2 fold before you can make the dc.

© All Copying Prohibited By Law

Likewise, when you are working across a row making a dc into each stitch in the previous row, don't stitch until you pass two cut ends together (one complete fold). Do not stitch between the half folds.

These directions are for working across rows. They do not apply at the beginning or end of a row or round.

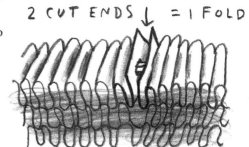

2 CUT ENDS ↓ = 1 FOLD

How two hands work together

Keep the folds pushed close to the hook end of the needle so they can be slipped off easily.

In the left hand, hold the work between the thumb and middle finger. The forefinger that holds the cord is extended. The left thumb separates the folds where the needle picks up the stitch from the previous row.

As the stitch is being made, the right-hand thumb, which rests on top of the folds on the needle, pushes the next fold toward the hook.

When the stitch is completed, the left-hand middle finger swings from the back of the work around to the front. With the thumb, it grasps the fold on the needle and pulls the fold off the needle.

As the fold is being released, a slight tug of the cord that lies over the left forefinger will tighten the tension of the stitch that was just completed. With practice you will do this automatically after each stitch. The left-hand middle finger returns to the back of the work, and you are ready to start the next stitch.

In the right hand, try to keep the folds of fabric pushed over the fingerhold to cushion the needle with fabric. Hold the needle in a relaxed way.

With practice you will develop an easy rhythm and learn to use your hands together in coordinated movements. With repetition, these finger movements become synchronized, and you will develop considerable speed.

© All Copying Prohibited By Law

Chapter Three

Making Shirrét

© All Copying Prohibited By Law

Putting it to use: Applying the basic rules to a real project

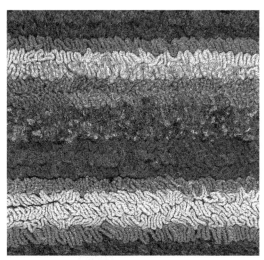

A little sampler. 5" x 5" in cotton, or 5¹⁄₂" x 5¹⁄₂" in wool

Rows

Square and rectangular shapes, which are made in rows, have great versatility. By working in rows you can make chair pads, long bench pads, long stair treads or stair carpeting, hall runners, wall hangings, pillows, and rugs of all sizes. You can make rugs with wide or narrow stripes, in solid colors or speckley patterns.

A little sampler is the perfect way to try your hand at making rows, the most basic of all Shirrét techniques.

You'll need 25 yards of Shirrét cord, marking pins, and a 27" (approximately) x 3/4" bias strip of each type of medium-weight fabric you'll be using.

You won't need big scraps for this project—just a variety. Look for wool or cotton (and they can be blended with polyester) fabric of medium thickness; avoid tightly woven percales or double knits or jeans. Work with one fabric per row—you'll start to see (and be surprised by) the unexpected look each different fabric has in Shirrét. If you make a wool and a cotton sampler you'll see the variety of elements you can "paint" with when you design later pieces.

Work back and forth in short horizontal rows. Fill the needle with 25 full folds, and cut strip. For the first three rows, use the longest strips you have. Since you have practiced the crochet stitches while learning to hold the Shirrét needle correctly, the Shirrét stitch will not be difficult for you. The Shirrét Sampler has the same starting row of chain stitches followed by rows of double crochet, but after every chain stitch you will pull a fold off the needle and onto the piece.

In the beginning two rows of every Shirrét, there is no base to work on and the stitches will twist and be unwieldy. Don't make the first row tight or perfect—just get it done. You need the first two rows as a base to practice on until you get the rhythm, so don't rip them out!

Fabric A. In the first row, each stitch is a chain stitch (ch st) and a fold.
Make a slip loop in the cord leaving 6" end.
Push folds forward on the needle close to the hook end.
Turn the strip over so cut end of strip near hook faces up, toward you.

© All Copying Prohibited By Law

Pull slip loop through this first 1/2 fold and on through next complete fold. Row has been started with 1¹/₂ folds.

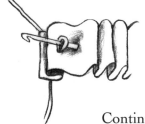

Continue as follows:

Make 1 ch st of cord and pull 1 fold from needle. *Make chain stitches very loose* because in the next row you will be working between these folds, and it will be difficult to get the hook between the folds if the ch sts are too tight.

When you have made 24 ch sts and pulled off 25 folds (plus the extra 1/2 fold at the starting end), you will end the row by cutting the strip of fabric. *The cord is never cut until the piece is finished; it holds the fabric together.*

Start of row looks like this:

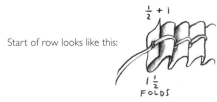

Slide the scissors through the center of the next fold on the needle. On top of the needle, cut through the strip.

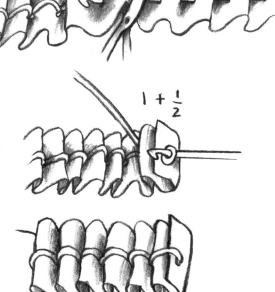

Pull this 1/2 fold off the needle, adding it to the fold already pulled off. The cut end will be facing you. Remember, when the cut end of a strip faces toward you, this is a half fold.

Make 1 ch st over last 1¹/₂ folds.

© All Copying Prohibited By Law

Row now has 24 ch sts and 24 folds (plus an extra 1/2 fold on each end). You are now ready to turn the ch st row over and work between the folds on the other side with double crochet stitches. All rows will be worked from right to left.

Make 2 ch sts of cord. This is a bridge.

Turn ch st over. Pull first 1½ folds from needle to start new row.

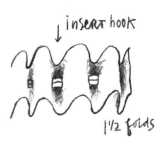

Skip first cord stitch and make 1 dc between 2nd and 3rd folds. Pull 1 fold from needle (1 Sh st completed).

There are 2 strands of cord between all folds and they are called a cord stitch. When you start a new row, skip the cord stitch between the 1st and 2nd folds. Insert the hook under the cord stitch between the 2nd and 3rd folds and make the first dc to start the new row. Pull 1 fold from needle. One Sh st completed.

Row 2: Fabric B. Continue across row with 1 Sh st in each cord stitch. The folds of fabric are now interlocked between the folds of the previous row. At the end of the row, make 1 dc between the last 2 folds and pull off 1 fold. Cut the strip on top of the needle in center of next fold and add this 1/2 fold to the fold already pulled off. The row ends with 1½ folds.

Congratulations! You've just completed the most difficult thing you'll ever do in Shirrét! The first two rows are awkward to do, so please don't rip anything out now! You've created a base to work on, and it's easier to Shirrét when you have 3+ rows that don't twist in your hands. Your very first Shirrét stitches may be too large and loose and they may show between rows, but relax. You'll get better faster by practicing on later rows, not the first three. You don't want your stitches to be too tight. Shirrét is relaxing.

© All Copying Prohibited By Law

Remember to breathe, and sit up straight and look around the garden once in a while to relax your eyes. You can be intense—but not too tense!

Row 3: Fabric C. Make a bridge (2 ch st) to the new row and turn the work over. Pull off 1¹/₂ folds to start new row.

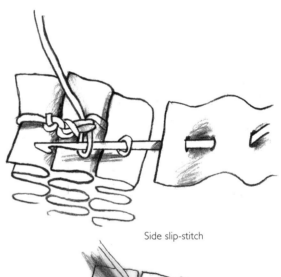

1¹/₂ folds

Skip the first cord st and make 1 dc between the 2nd and 3rd folds. Continue across row with 1 Sh st in each cord stitch.

Each row ends with 1 dc between the last two folds, and 1¹/₂ folds from the needle.

Before you turn around to start back, insert the hook under the cord stitches that are along the side of the end fold. Cord over hook, pull through loop and on through the loop on the needle. This slip stitch, at the end of each row, should be a long, loose loop. Its purpose is to carry the cord in a continuous row of stitches along both sides of the piece. These stitches are usually covered by a border or adjacent patchwork pieces, and bordered.

Side slip-stitch

Make a bridge (ch 2), turn the work.

Row 4: Fabric D, and following 10 rows, fabric E, F etc. Fill the needle with 25 full folds of the next color. Repeat 3rd row (Pull first 1¹/₂ folds from needle. Make 1 dc between 2nd and 3rd folds of previous row, continue.)

Don't be concerned about your workmanship at this stage. With practice you'll learn to make double crochet stitches the right size, thus pulling the rows close together. The really important thing for now is to practice to get a feel for

© All Copying Prohibited By Law

the basic process. The fingers will soon do their work automatically without conscious guidance from you.

> *If you've made a wool sampler,* measure it after row 14. If it is $5^1/2$", you are finished. In wool, a row is about 3/8" high, so it will take approximately 15 rows to make a $5^1/2$" x $5^1/2$" square.
>
> *If your sampler is cotton,* a row is 1/4" high approximately and 16 rows will make a 5" x 5" square. After the last stitch, leave 6" of cord and cut it. Then pull the cord through the loop on the hook and tighten.

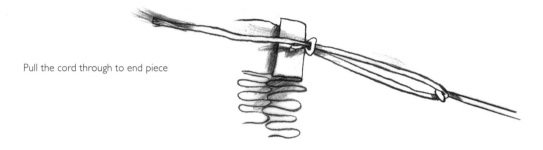

Pull the cord through to end piece

Adding borders

After completing the horizontal rows of a square or rectangular piece, you will add a border to the outside edges to cover the cord stitches that show on the outsides and chain stitch end.

  The border is several rows encircling the piece, and is thus called a "round" because it is not a spiral, but a square or circle that meets itself and appears to have no beginning or end. Each round of the border is a complete unit, with a bridge to the next level so you can change color without an unsightly jog in the design. In a square or rectangle, the Shirrét stitches are one for one except for the corners, when increase stitches are made, and the final round.

> **Round 1**: Color A. Ch 2 and turn the work. Work back across row just completed. In last cord stitch of row, pull off 4 folds to turn the corner. Mark location by pinning these 4 folds together. Do not cut the strip.

© All Copying Prohibited By Law

To determine the number of stitches to make on the sides of a square, count the number of rows in the piece, add half again as many, and make that the total number of folds and stitches.

Example: If there are 40 horizontal rows, add an extra 20 (half the number of rows) for a total of 60 stitches to be picked up along the side edge. Pick up the same number along the opposite side to keep the piece uniform. Pin mark the side in quarters before starting to pick up stitches in order to distribute the stitches evenly. Folds should be approximately the same distance apart along the sides as in the horizontal rows.

There aren't any fold spaces to go into along the sides, so you make stitches into the cord with the same spacing as in a regular row of Shirrét, with dc stitches. According to the formula, we'll make 28 Shirrét stitches (+1/2 fold on each end), so at the quarter point you've done 7, at the center 14, and at 3/4 - 21. In the last st of this side, pull off 4 folds for corner. Pin folds together to mark location.

Continue across ch st row, making 1 regular Sh st in every ch st. Pull off 4 folds in last ch st to turn corner. Pin folds together to mark location.

For next side, repeat procedure of picking up sts same as second side. Be sure to have same number of sts — 28 — and folds (+1/2 at each end) as second side to keep piece uniform. In last st pull off 4 folds.

Then cut strip on top of needle and add extra 1/2 fold so rnd ends with 4½ folds. Complete rnd with slip stitch through the bridge. (Insert hook under bridge, cord over hook, pull through a loop and on through the loop on the needle). Put pin marker through last fold before slip stitch to mark end of first rnd.

Round 2: Color B. In this rnd, increases will be made in each corner to add extra fullness. An increase is made by pulling off 2 folds instead of 1 fold after the double crochet stitch. To start the new rnd, make a bridge and pull off 1½ folds. Skip first cord stitch and continue with regular Sh st. At each corner where 4 folds are pin marked together, make 1 inc in each of the 2 center cord sts and pin the folds together to establish corner location for next rnd. At end of rnd cut strip and complete with a slip st through the bridge. Transfer pin marker from last fold of previous rnd to last fold of this rnd.

Round 3: Color C. Repeat rnd 2.

Round 4: Color D. Final rnd. At each corner where the 4 folds are pin marked, make 1 dc and pull off 4 folds in one of the center cord sts and repeat in next cord st. Then pull off 2 folds in every other stitch until the next corner. The corners are increases, but the rest is treated as a final rnd.

For a firm finished edge, 2 folds are pulled off in every other stitch. This fills in the spaces between the cord stitches. Folds will be quite close together.

© All Copying Prohibited By Law

Begin and end all strips with the cut ends turned to the inside, or center, of the work (the cut ends should be facing you on the top or front of the needle so they will turn inside when attached to the piece). If a strip falls with the cut end to the outside (on the back of the needle, not facing you), cut off the extra 1/2 fold.

If the fabric used for the final round has a definite right and wrong side, be sure the right side is turned to the outside (on the back of the needle, not facing you) for an attractive finish. If you are careful to fill your needle with the ends of strips matched to turn inside (facing you on top of the needle) and the right side of the fabric turned to the outside (on the back of the needle), it will save time and possible mistakes when you attach the final round. *Remember: The wrong side of the fabric will be facing you on the needle because the folds turn over after they are attached.*

At the end of the round, cut strip, add the extra 1/2 fold. Fasten with slip stitch (insert hook under bridge, cord over hook, pull through a loop and on through loop of the slip stitch). Work end back into piece, fasten securely several times, and cut off excess.

To determine the width of a square or rectangular piece, make the starting chain stitch row the width you want your finished piece to be, subtract the width of the border (times 2 for 2 sides). It is advisable to make the chain stitch row a little shorter than the finished width you want. If necessary, an additional round of border can be added to reach the finished size. Determine the number of rows to make by subtracting the width of the border (times 2) from the finished size.

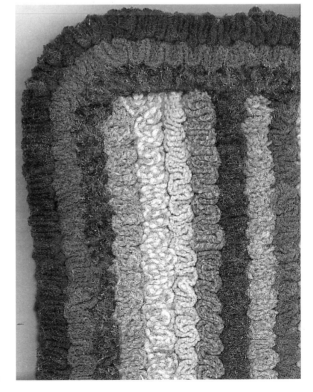

The doubled strips of this chair pad create visual interest *and* add firmness.

© All Copying Prohibited By Law

Helpful hints: Maintaining even rows by counting folds

To keep a square or rectangular piece symmetrical, it is important that you maintain the same number of folds in every row. Count the folds as you fill the needle.

To know how many folds there are per row in a square or rectangle, look back at the starting chain stitch row and count the chain stitches as they round over the folds and add one. Adding one allows for the extra 1/2 fold at the beginning and end of each row. This is the number of double crochet stitches you will make in each of the following rows, and the number of folds you will attach. Example: If you have 10 sts in the chain stitch row, fill your needle with 11 complete folds so you'll have an extra 1/2 fold for each end. Each space between two folds, where there are two strands of cord, is a stitch. Count those up, and you know you always have on fold more.

If the piece is getting wider, you are adding extra folds by forgetting to skip the first cord stitch when you start each new row. If the piece is getting narrower, you are losing folds. You may be making a dc st and forgetting to pull off a fold afterward. Look back into your crochet stitches. If you find dc sts together without a fold between, the row will be short a fold. Remember: There must be a fold of fabric after every stitch.

You may be forgetting to pull off 1½ folds after the bridge at the start of each new row. You may be ending the row with a dc st and forgetting to pull off the 1½ folds that go with it. Or, you may be ending the row too soon in the 2nd to last stitch, and failing to work all the way to the end of the row.

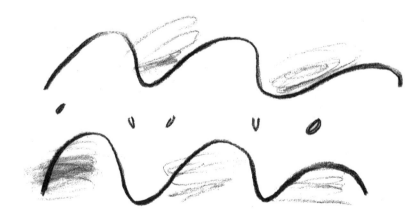

© All Copying Prohibited By Law

Patchwork Shirrét

An attractive use for scraps and remnants is to make sampler squares without a border. As you finish a sampler, work across the last row of folds with cord only, no folds, and make a single crochet stitch between each fold. Cut the cord and leave a 14" length to be used later to lace pieces together. Thread a blunt tapestry needle with one of the cord lengths. Push needle down through a cord stitch on one piece and up through a cord stitch on adjoining piece. As the lacing thread is pulled up snugly, the two pieces will blend together with no sign of a join. Lace through all the edges: starting chain stitch row, row of crochet stitches across the top, and/or the exposed cord along the sides. When all the pieces are laced together, work with Shirrét stitches around all four sides for a border of one, two or three rows.

When you're planning it, think of beautiful and surprising color transitions. People are mystified by patchwork Shirrét; they can't figure out how it's made!

The small squares of patchwork make it a great carry-along project for commuting and traveling!

Helpful hints: Adjusting the size of folds and stitches

If your finished work is considerably larger than the sizes given for the patterns, you may be making your shirred folds too large as you thread the needle. You may also be making your crochet stitches too loose. When you insert the needle under the cord stitch to bring up the third loop of the double crochet stitch, keep the third loop down inside the fold. Bringing this third loop up high near the top of the fold results in a tall, loose stitch, and your Shirrét will not have as much body as it would with a smaller, firmer stitch.

© All Copying Prohibited By Law

Keeping a written log

A simple, reliable method for keeping track of your Shirrét projects is to keep a notebook, or log.

Round	Start	End
1	✔	✔
2	✔	✔
3	✔	✔
4	✔	

Make notes as you go along. You may want to include details like the size and shape of the piece, or the fabrics used for it (Juliet's favorite dress, Lovis's blue jeans, sofa slipcover). If new fabric is used, indicate where purchased, the yardage and price. It is interesting to keep a sample swatch of each fabric used. Staple a small piece in the notebook, labeled Color A, Color B, etc., so you can identify the finished effect in your piece. If special handling was given, such as soaking in fabric softener, pre-washing, etc., make a note of it. If you find a given fabric is difficult to work with, or think it might have been easier to handle with soaking, write it down. Write down everything that might be helpful in the future.

If you have divided your yardage or old clothing into separate pieces, record how many rows or rounds were made from each bag of strips. Keep a complete record, round by round: the number of folds in chain stitch row; increase rounds, along with any notes as to whether piece was cupped or rippled before or after the round; where color changes were made; if a design is used, a sketch or graph, or description.

The log is particularly useful when making round or oval Shirrét. While it is important to keep an accurate count of folds for the first three rounds of the center, once the piece is well established, it is not necessary to continue this exact counting. A missed fold here and there will not be crucial in a room-size rug! However, it is important to keep an accurate record of your rounds as you go along so you so you will not miss an increase round. With round and oval pieces, it is important to make increase rounds in the proper order, especially in the beginning when the piece is small. If you don't keep track, you may forget where you left off and make increase rounds too close together, or miss one completely.

When a piece is completed, include a final note with the date and finished size. Record the amount of yardage used and estimated cord required. You will have a detailed history—or "herstory!"—of your piece. Then, because it is often a source of pleasure and pride to identify your work with a name, perhaps you will bestow a title on your finished Shirrét!

© All Copying Prohibited By Law

© All Copying Prohibited By Law

Rounds

After you have learned the basic technique by making a square or rectangular piece, the next step is to make a round Shirrét. The same basic rules of Shirrét apply, and your newfound ability to use the needle will make it easy for you to start the round center. All the basic steps you need for round Shirrét were illustrated in row Shirrét.

Pattern: Round center

Regardless of the fabric used or the finished size desired, all round pieces start with the following procedure. The first 3 rounds are increase rounds because it is necessary to pull off 2 folds with each stitch to establish the round shape. The piece starts with a short chain stitch row that is then fastened together with a slip stitch to form a ring of folds for the first round of the center. Work continues around this center. Each round is *connected* by slip stitching the end of the round onto the beginning…thus, each round is a complete unit. The strip of fabric on the needle is not cut until the end of the third round, at which time the center has been completed.

> **Materials:** An extra needle, filled ahead, helps to get an accurate count of folds when you're making centers or increase rounds. Stitchmaking is a bit smoother using extra needles that have been filled ahead of time.
>
> It is very important to have the correct number of specified folds in each of the first 3 rounds. There will be $12^{1}/_{2}$ folds in the starting chain stitch row, which becomes the first round. There will be 24 folds in the second round, and 48 folds (plus an extra 1/2 fold when the strip is cut at the end of the round) in the third round.
>
> It is recommended that you make these first 3 rounds as a sample before starting the center of a finished piece. Using a firm-bodied cotton or wool for practice will make it easier for you to count the folds accurately.

Round 1.

1. Make slip loop in cord, leaving 6" end.

2. Turn fabric strip on needle so cut end faces you. Pull slip loop through this first 1/2 fold and on through next 2 folds. Ch st row has been started with $2^{1}/_{2}$ folds.

Chain stitch first row to make center

© All Copying Prohibited By Law

3. Make 1 ch st and pull off next 2 folds. Make ch sts loose. Continue pulling off 2 folds after each ch st until there are 6 ch sts and 12 folds (plus extra 1/2 fold on starting end). Do not cut the strip.

4. With left thumb, roll ch st row just completed to the right toward the needle. Turn the $2\frac{1}{2}$ folds and the tail of cord that started the row inside the ring of folds so chain stitches are completely hidden. Insert needle under both threads of the cord stitch that is between the first and second folds on the back side of the ch st row.

5. Cord over hook and pull loop through cord stitch and on through loop on hook. You now have a tight little ring of 12 folds fastened together with a slip stitch. Tighten tension of sl st to draw beginning and end of rnd close together.

6. To mark the end of the 1st rnd, put a pin marker after the last (12th) fold pulled off. Put pin halfway between that fold and the next fold that is still on the needle. Pin through single thickness of fabric through lower half so pin hangs down.

Slip Stitch the chain stitch row and mark round center

Round 2.

In this rnd you will be pulling off 2 folds after every dc st, for a total of 24 folds. A helpful little trick to make sure that you have attached the correct number of folds by the end of the rnd is to *count ahead the folds on your needle, and put a pin marker after the 24th fold*. Start counting the first fold after the pin that marks the end of the first rnd. Be sure to match up cut ends of strips in complete folds. Place a pin marker halfway between the 24th fold and the next fold on the needle. When you attach the folds, this pin should fall at the correct place to end the 2nd rnd.

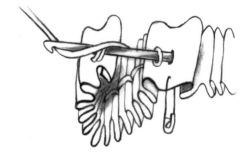

Second round of center—double crochet

PIN JUST AFTER the 24th FOLD

© All Copying Prohibited By Law

1. Make 2 ch sts (bridge) to raise to level of new rnd. Pull off 2 folds.

2. Continue around the center, making 1 dc st and pulling off 2 folds in each cord stitch. Rnd ends with 1 dc plus 2 folds in the last cord stitch before the pin marking the end of the 1st rnd. Do not cut the strip.

3. If you did not count the 24 folds ahead, count them now. Count either the folds, or count the cord stitches between the folds. If you count folds, start with the fold that has the pin marking end of first rnd. If you count cord stitches, start with the first one to the left of the pin marking end of 1st rnd. Count folds or cord stitches *before* the rnd is slip stitched together.

4. If you counted your 24 folds ahead, the pin after the 24th fold should be in the correct place to mark the end of this second rnd. If not, look back into your crochet sts to be sure you worked into every cord st, and that you pulled off 2 folds after every stitch. The folds of the first rnd are rather close together, and you must be careful to separate every fold to avoid missing a stitch.

5. When you are sure that you have attached 24 folds, insert hook under cord stitch to left of pin marking end of first rnd. Make slip stitch to pull beginning and end of this rnd together.

6. Transfer pin marker from first rnd to end of second rnd. Pin through single thickness of fabric halfway between 24th fold and next fold still on needle. Tie a small piece of red string or yarn to head of pin to make it easily visible.

Round 3.

In this round you will again be pulling off 2 folds after every stitch for a total of 48 folds (plus an extra 1/2 fold when the round ends). This round completes the center, so you will cut the strip when the round ends. If you wish to count ahead, the total number of folds to be attached will be 48$^1/_2$ folds.

1. Make bridge to third rnd and pull off 2 folds.

2. Continue around with 1 dc and 2 folds in each cord stitch. Rnd ends in last stitch before the pin which marks the end of the 2nd rnd. Count folds to be sure you have attached a total of 48 in this rnd.

© All Copying Prohibited By Law

3. Cut strip on top of needle in center of next fold. Pull off this 1/2 fold. Rnd ends with 2½ folds.

4. Slip stitch through cord stitch which is to the left of pin marker. Transfer pin marker from second rnd to end of this third rnd. Now that you have cut the strip, you will have a complete fold at the end of each round. Pin through the double thickness of the fold.

The 3 rounds just completed constitute the center of a round shape. Follow this procedure for all round pieces. It is necessary to pull off 2 folds with every stitch to get the round center established. But *once the center has been completed, never increase in every stitch again.* Follow the increase schedules given with individual patterns that follow.

To continue, use the pattern for the table mat and the chair pad that follows.

Round 3 completes the center of any round piece

Pattern: Round to 8" *Table Mat*

This table mat is an excellent project to develop skill working "in the round." You will learn how to make increases to keep the piece flat, and how to make connected rounds and how to bridge. The mat works up quickly, and you can then advance to chair pads and round rugs. Colors can be arranged any way you like, but this pattern is written with the center and all increase rounds made with Color A, and the regular rounds with Color B. This will make it easy to keep track of increase rounds.

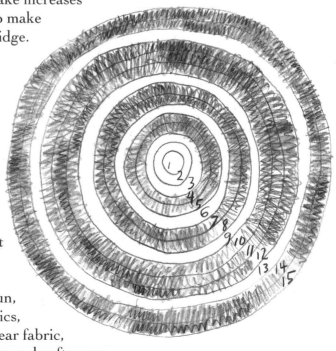

Materials: Medium-weight woven fabric such as cotton or polyester blended duck, homespun, drapery or curtain fabrics, outing flannel, sportswear fabric, wrinkle cloth. Use denim only after you have completed your first round Shirrét.

© All Copying Prohibited By Law

Color A: 1/4 yd. 36"-45" fabric
Color B: 1/2 yd. 36"-45" fabric
Cord: Approx. 100 yds. Marking pins
Increase rnds: marked*. Follow directions given.
Regular rnds: No increasing.

To start center: Color A. Follow instructions for first 3 rounds.

Round 4.

Regular rnd. Change to Color B. From the 4th round on, every round in Shirrét is a connected round, and at the end of the connected round, there is a bridge that takes you up to the next level.

It is because of connected rounds and bridges that the designs of Shirrét rugs have a professional and sophisticated appearance. *Round Shirrét is made of concentric circles instead of spirals.* When the color changes, you don't see an overlap at the spot where one color is dropped and a new one starts. The bridge that allows the color change is hidden in the middle of the folds of fabric. This is a great advantage provided by the Shirrét technique, because it allows complete freedom in the choice of colors and color placement for color bands. Designs will always be "in register."

Because of connected rounds, your Shirrét has a finished appearance at the end of every round. You can use your Shirrét until the next time you add to it! Use it as a hot mat, then make it into a chair pad, then a small rug and finally a room size rug. It won't ever be another unfinished needlework project in a closet!

1. Make 2 ch sts of cord. This is the bridge that raises to the level of the new round. Turn fabric strip on needle so cut end of strip faces toward you. Pull loop of cord through cut end of strip and on through next complete fold. Thus, 1½ folds are pulled off the needle after the bridge to start the new round.

2. Insert hook under the threads of the cord stitch between the first and second folds and make 1 dc. *On this fourth rnd only make dc between first and second folds and pull off 1 fold.*

3. Continue around with Shirrét stitch (1 dc plus 1 fold) in every cord st. Rnd ends in last cord st before pin marker (total of 48 folds).

4. Cut strip. Rnd ends with 1½ folds.

© All Copying Prohibited By Law

5. Connect rnd as follows:
    Insert hook under bridge that
    started this rnd. Cord over hook and
    pull loop under bridge and on
    through loop on hook. Slip stitch
    completed.

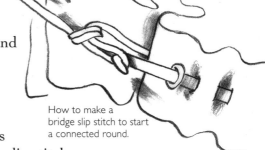

How to make a
bridge slip stitch to start
a connected round.

6. Transfer pin marker from previous
    round to last fold pulled off before slip stitch.

Round 5.

Regular (connected) rnd. Continue with Color B.

1. Make bridge (2 ch sts of cord) and pull off 1½ folds.

2. Skip first cord stitch. Make dc st *between the 2nd and 3rd folds* and pull 1
    fold from needle.

3. Continue around with Shirrét stitch (1 dc and 1 fold) between each
    fold of the previous round.

To end a connected round, follow these steps:

1. Round ends in last cord stitch before the pin marker at the end of the
    round.

2. Make 1 dc and pull off 1 fold (or 2 folds if an increase round).

3. Cut the strip that is on the needle. Cut on top of needle in center of
    next fold. This gives an extra 1/2 fold.

4. Pull off this 1/2 fold, adding it to the fold already pulled off. Round
    ends with 1½ folds (or 2½ folds if an increase round).

5. Fasten round with slip stitch to pull beginning and end of round
    together.

6. Transfer pin marker from previous round to last fold pulled off before
    slip stitch. *Note: It is helpful to tie a short piece of red string or yarn to head of
    marking pin to signal "stop" at the end of the round.*

Note that all rounds will follow the above procedure, and each round is a
connect and bridge round.

© All Copying Prohibited By Law

*Round 6.

Increase rnd. Change to Color A. Extra fullness must be added in this rnd to keep work flat. Increases will be made by pulling off 2 folds after every other stitch. The easiest way to keep the increase pattern accurate is to count the first stitch as #1 and pull off 1 fold, the next stitch as #2 and pull off 2 folds. Repeat this formula as you continue around. If you lose count, look back into the crochet stitches to determine whether you pulled off 1 or 2 folds last.

1. Make bridge and pull off $1\frac{1}{2}$ folds (count "1").

2. Skip first cord stitch. Make 1 dc in next st and pull off 2 folds (count "2").

3. Make 1 dc in next st and pull off 1 fold (count "1").

4. Make 1 dc in next st and pull off 2 fold (count "2").

5. Continue around in this manner. Last st of rnd should be an increase st, so pull off 2 folds. Cut strip, add the extra 1/2 fold. Rnd ends with $2\frac{1}{2}$ folds. Connect rnd.

6. Total number of folds should be 72 (48 folds plus 24 folds added this increase rnd).

7th Rnd: Regular rnd. Change to Color B.
8th Rnd: Regular rnd. Continue with Color B.
9th Rnd: Increase rnd. Change to Color A.
Increases for this rnd will be made in every other stitch. Follow same procedure as 6th Rnd. Total folds by end of round should be 108.

Note: Should your piece "cup" slightly or if the center should "bump", do not be concerned if you have made the increase rnds in the correct order, and have also determined that you have the exact number of folds. The benefit of extra folds added on an increase rnd will not be derived until you have worked into these extra folds on the next rnd. The piece may continue to cup a bit for 1 or 2 rnds, but will usually flatten out by the 3rd round.

10th Rnd: Regular rnd. Change to Color B.
11th Rnd: Regular rnd. Continue with Color B.
12th Rnd: Regular rnd. Continue with Color B.
13th Rnd: Increase rnd. Change to Color A.
Increase in every other stitch. Total folds at end of rnd should be 162.
14th Rnd: Regular rnd. Change to Color B.
15th Rnd: Color B. Final round

© All Copying Prohibited By Law

Note: If you wish to make a larger size piece, omit the final round and continue with Rnd 15 in the larger round chair pad pattern that follows.

For a firm finished edge, pull off 2 folds with every other stitch. This will fill in the spaces between cord stitches. Folds will be quite close together. Begin and end all strips with the cut ends turned to the inside of the work. If a strip falls with the cut end to the outside, cut off the extra 1/2 fold. If the fabric used for the final round has a definite right and wrong side, be sure right side is turned to the outside for an attractive finish. If you are careful to fill your needle with the ends of strips matched to turn to the inside, and the right side to the outside, it will save time and possible mistakes when attaching the final round. Remember: The wrong side of the strips will be facing you as you attach them, because the folds turn over after they are attached.

At the end of the round, cut the strip, and add the extra 1/2 fold. Fasten with slip stitch through bridge. Cut cord and pull end through loop of the slip stitch. Work end back into piece, fasten securely several times and cut off excess.

Pattern: Round to 14 1/2"
Chair pad in cotton

Materials: Medium-weight woven fabric
    such as cotton or polyester blended
    sportswear fabrics, duck, denim.
Background: 7/8 yd. 45" fabric
Color A: 3/8 yd. 45" fabric
Color B: 5/8 yd. 45" fabric
Cord: approximately 200 yds.
Marking Pins
Color Pattern:
Center through 9th round: background fabric
Rnds 10, 11, 12: Color A
Rnds 13, 14, 15, 16: background fabric
Rnds 17, 18, 19: Color B
Rnds 20, 21, 22, 23: background fabric
Rnds 24, 25, 26: Color A
Rnds 27, 28, 29: Color B

Center through 14th rnd: Follow pattern for 8" Round table mat.
Rnds 15 - 18: Regular rounds.
19th rnd: Increase *in every other stitch*. Total folds at end of round should
    be 243.
Rnds 20 - 27: Regular rounds.

© All Copying Prohibited By Law

28th rnd: Increase in *every third stitch*. Count 1, 2, 3; 1, 2, 3.
   On each count of 3, pull off 2 folds for the increase. Total
   folds at end of
   round should be 324.
29th rnd: Final round.

For a larger chair pad, add more rounds to size required, with increase
rounds if necessary.
   Block the piece so it lays flat.

Helpful hints: How to increase properly

Increasing, which keeps your rugs from cupping or rippling, is done by adding an extra fold to the stitch. The secret of increasing success is to do it the right amount at the right time. Increase rounds must be made often enough to keep the piece lying flat, but not so often as to result in ruffling of the edges. Lay your work down every several rounds to determine if it needs an increase round.

The weight and bulk of the fabric determines how often to increase. That means that increases are different for cotton and wool, for lightweight and heavy fabrics. Other determining factors are individual differences in stitch size and tension, and the differences in the size of the shirred folds.

After the initial increase rounds of the center and the early rounds, which you will follow in the patterns in this book up to 14" size, it is usually necessary to work at least three rounds after an increase round before it is time to increase again. When you notice that the folds are getting farther apart, with more of the cord showing between the folds, it is time to increase. When you notice that the outside round is beginning to turn in slightly toward the center, or when you notice that the outside round is actually beginning to turn up a bit like the rim of a saucer, it is time to increase! These are signs that the outside round is too small for the growing diameter, and more folds are needed.

After an increase round has been made, the effect of the extra fullness of added folds will not be evident for several rounds. Do not increase again immediately. If an increase round is repeated too soon, ruffling will result! So be sure to work for several rounds before increasing again. You may notice that the piece cups slightly for one or two rounds after an increase round. Don't worry! It will usually flatten out by the third round.

© All Copying Prohibited By Law

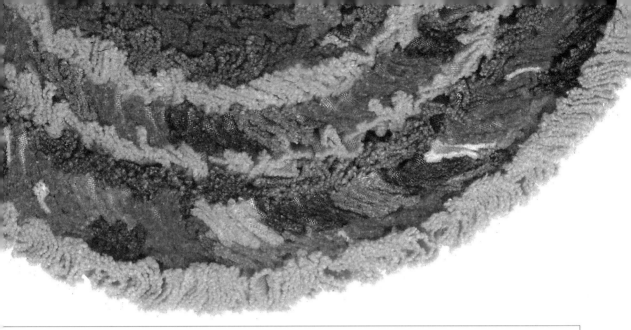

As a Shirrét piece gets larger, less increasing is needed. Increase rounds are spaced farther apart, and within each increase round, the increases are spaced farther apart.

To increase, make one crochet stitch of cord and pull off two folds of fabric, instead of one fold.

Do not make two double crochet stitches in one cord stitch.

Do not increase in every stitch after the center has been completed.

Always make increases in one given round to maintain the symmetry of a piece.

Always make increases in even increments. That is, in *every* stitch to start the center of a round or oval piece; in every *other* stitch in the early rounds; and in every *third* stitch as the piece gets larger. Then in every fourth stitch, fifth stitch, sixth stitch, etc.

Increase in every third stitch in a given round, and then increase in every third stitch *again* when the next increase round is made. The next increase round will be in every fourth stitch, and again in every fourth stitch for the next increase round. Then increase in every fifth stitch, repeating it one more time, etc.

Continue this pattern until the piece is completed.

When Shirrét gets large, the edges may start to ripple several rounds after increasing. This extra fullness will usually work out in subsequent rounds. However, if the edge is rippled near the final finishing round, take out the extra fullness by decreasing. This is done by skipping folds in the same sequence as the last increase round (skip every fourth, skip every fifth, or skip every sixth as the case may be), or use your judgment as to how much decreasing is required. Decreasing is only done if there is too much fullness at the outer edge when you are ready to finish off.

© All Copying Prohibited By Law

Ovals

An oval Shirrét is really an adaptation of the round shape. The difference is that the increasing is done only on the oval ends, rather than evenly spaced all around, as in a round piece. To keep the ends symmetrical, the increases must be distributed evenly all around the end. This is done by finding the halfway point in the center of the end. Called the center top (CT), this point is marked by a pin. There should always be an equal number of increases on the right and left side of the CT, and both ends of the oval must also be identical in size and shape.

The first end is the end arrived at first after starting each new round, while the second end is the last end worked around before the round comes to an end. The 6" tail of cord that starts the chain stitch row will help to identify the second end.

Remember: If you make increases on one side of the oval end, you must make the same number of increases on the other side of the oval end to keep the piece symmetrical from side to side. And if you make increases on the first end of the oval shape, you must make increases on the second end to keep the piece symmetrical from end to end.

It takes five rounds to establish the center of an oval piece. Regardless of the fabric used or the finished size, all oval pieces start with this procedure. Rules 1 and 2, which you used on the square and round pieces, also apply to the oval shape. It is especially important to remember Rule #1 when increasing on the oval ends. When you count back from the CT to make the first increase, be sure to make the double crochet stitch *first* and then pull off two folds to add to the stitch for the first increase.

The first round will be made in two steps. First is the chain stitch row, which establishes the first half of the center. The length of the starting chain stitch row determines the proportional shape of the finished piece. The second step is working back along the chain stitch row to form the other half of the center. This first round is then connected with a slip stitch, and work continues around this oval center.

Pattern: 7" x 10" Oval Table Mat

This oval mat, which is an attractive and useful hot dish mat to use under platters and casseroles, will help teach you how to start the center of an oval piece and turn the ends with increases. The pattern is written with every other round of the center and the increase rounds made with Color A. Alternate rounds of the center and all regular rounds are made with Color B. This will make it easy to keep track of the rounds. Keep a written record of work in progress, checking off each round as it is completed.

Materials: Medium-weight woven cotton or blended fabrics such as denim, duck.

Color A: 3/8 yd. 45" fabric
Color B: 3/8 yd. 45" fabric
Cord: approx 100 yds.
Marking pins
Before starting, tie a 4" piece of red yarn or string to the head of one of the marking pins. This red pin will be used to mark the end of each round. Tie green yarn to the head of 2 pins to mark the center top of the first end. Tie yellow string to the head of 2 pins to mark the second end.

Round 1 of center: chain stitch row. Color A. If you wish to fill your needle with the exact number of folds in advance, it will require 36 complete folds to complete this rnd.

X = 2 fold increase

2ND End YELLOW pin

TRANSFER YELLOW pin

PERmanenT YELLOW pin

End of connected rounds and Bridge

RED pin

2 Chain stitches

STaRTiNG CH ST Row - 14½

PErmanenT GREEN pin

TRansfer GREEN pin

1ST End GREEN PIN

1. Make slip loop in cord, leaving 6" end, and pull through 1½ folds to start. Continue with 1 ch st of cord and 1 fold until ch st row has 14 ch sts and 14 folds, plus the extra ½ fold on the starting end.

© All Copying Prohibited By Law

2. After 14th ch st, pull off 2 folds (1st inc). Make 2 ch sts and pull off 2 more folds (2nd inc). Put the green pin through single thickness of fabric halfway between the 2 increases (below the 2 ch sts) so pin hangs down. This is a permanent marker and should remain in place until mat is finished to mark location of the CT of this first end.

Do not turn the work. Instead of turning the ch st row over, as in the square piece, you will now work back from right to left along the ch st row just completed. It will require 15 folds to work to the center of the second end, so it will be helpful to count ahead the next 15 folds on the needle, and put the yellow pin halfway between the 15th and 16th folds.

Completing center: Notice that your starting ch st row has a single strand of cord over the center of each fold, and a small knot between the folds. You will insert your hook under the knot for each dc st as you work back along the ch st row. Keep the loops of your dc sts small to pull these two halves of the center round close together for a firm center.

1. Skip the first knot, which is between the 2 increases. Cord over and insert hook under the next knot, which is between the first inc that was made to turn the end and the next single fold. Make 1 dc and pull off 1 fold.

2. Continue, making 1 dc and pulling off 1 fold in the next 13 knots between the folds. In the 14th (final) knot of the row, make 1 dc and pull off 2 folds (1st inc of second end). Make 2 ch sts and pull off 2 folds for the second inc. The yellow pin should be halfway between the 2 increases (below the 2 ch sts) through single thickness of fabric. This permanent pin marks the CT of this second end.

3. Complete rnd by cutting the strip on top of needle and adding the extra 1/2 fold to the 2 folds of the second inc. Rnd ends with $2\frac{1}{2}$ folds.

4. With left thumb, push the $1\frac{1}{2}$ folds and tail of cord that started the ch st row completely over, so ch st row is hidden. Insert hook under the cord stitch that is between the first and second folds on the back side of the ch st row. Make slip st to draw beginning and end of rnd

© All Copying Prohibited By Law

together. Put red pin through last
fold pulled off before the
slip st. This pin
marks the end of the
first rnd.

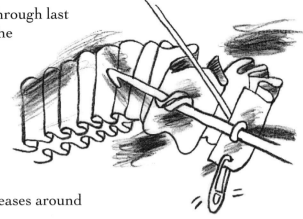

Round 2 of center (4 increases around
each end). Color B.
For this and all following round, a regular Shirrét
Stitch is used - 1 dc st *plus* 1 fold (or 2 folds when an increase is called
for). This second rnd will require 43 complete folds (42 folds plus 2
half folds).

1. Make bridge (2 ch sts) to raise to level of new rnd. Pull off $1\frac{1}{2}$
    folds and *skip first cord stitch*. Continue down the side with regular
    Shirrét stitch.

2. Nearing the first end, look ahead to the green pin that marks the CT.
    In the 2nd cord stitch before the green pin, make 1 dc and pull off 2
    folds (1st inc). Repeat in next cord st. You should now be up to the
    permanent green pin. Put your second green pin through single
    thickness of strip halfway between the last fold just pulled off and
    next fold which is still on the needle. Pin through bottom of strip so
    pin hangs down.

3. Make 1 inc in each of the next 2 cord sts after the pin marker. First
    end has now been turned with a total of 4 inc (2 before pin at CT and
    2 after it).

4. Continue down the second side with regular Shirrét stitch.

5. Repeat #2 and #3 to turn the second end. If you started the first inc
    in the correct place, the fourth inc should come in the last cord st of
    the rnd, just before the red pin marking the end of the rnd. Cut strip
    and add the extra 1/2 fold. Rnd ends with $2\frac{1}{2}$ folds. Connect rnd in
    usual way. Transfer red pin from last fold of previous rnd to last fold
    of this rnd.

***Note: If you lose count or want to check what you have done, separate the rounds
and look back into the stitches. You can easily count how many folds have been
pulled off after each stitch.***

© All Copying Prohibited By Law

Round 3 of center (8 increases each end). Color A.

For this rnd it will be necessary to reverse the direction of working around the oval center in order to maintain the position of the pin markers at CT of each end. It will require 59 folds (58 folds plus 1 half fold on each end) to complete the rnd.

1. Make bridge. Turn piece around so you are working toward the end with the yellow pin. The pin markers and the tail of cord from the starting ch st row will be on the opposite side.

2. You will be increasing in 8 sts around each end, so pull off 2½ folds (1st inc). *Skip first cord stitch*. Inc in next 3 sts. You are now at the yellow pin marking the CT. Transfer this pin from the previous rnd. Pin through single thickness of strip halfway between last fold pulled off and next fold still on needle.

3. Make 1 inc in each of next 4 cord sts. End has been turned with 8 inc, and the yellow pin is halfway between.

4. Continue down side with regular Shirrét stitch.

5. To turn the second end, make first inc in the fourth cord stitch before CT. Make 4 inc. Transfer green pin from previous rnd, and make 4 more inc. Rnd ends in the last st before the bridge. Because this rnd was worked in a reverse direction, the red pin marking the end of the rnd will be on the left side of the bridge. Connect rnd with slip st and transfer red pin.

Round 4 of center (10 increases each end). Color B.

This rnd will be worked in the normal direction. You will be working on the side that has the tail of cord and the permanent pin markers. It will require 79 folds to complete the rnd.

1. Make bridge and turn piece around. Pull off 1½ folds and skip first cord stitch. Work along the side (toward the green pin) with Shirrét stitch. Make first inc in the fifth cord st before CT. After the fifth inc, transfer green pin from previous rnd, and then make 5 more inc on the other side of pin.

2. Continue along side with regular Shirrét stitch.

3. Repeat same increase procedure at the second end. After completing the tenth inc, there should be 3 cord sts left in which to make regular Shirrét stitch.

© All Copying Prohibited By Law

4. Round ends with 1½ folds. Connect rnd and transfer red pin.

Round 5 of center (12 increases in each end). Color A.
   This round will be worked in the reverse direction, the same as the third rnd. It requires 103 folds.

1. Make bridge and turn piece around so you are working toward the yellow end. Pull off 1½ folds and skip first cord stitch. Continue with 6 regular Shirrét stitches.

2. Increase in next 12 sts around the end. After making the 6th inc (which should fall in the st before the yellow pin), transfer the pin and make 6 more inc after the pin.

3. Continue along the side with regular Sh st. Make 12 inc around the green end, starting first inc in the sixth cord st before pin marker. Transfer pin after the 6th inc.

4. Continue along 2nd side with regular Sh st.

5. Rnd ends with 1½ folds. Connect rnd and transfer red pin.

   This completes the center. You will have 5 pin markers in the work: 2 green pins at the first end, 2 yellow pins at the second end, and a red pin marking the end of the round. The only marker you will continue to transfer from round to round is the red pin marking the last fold before the bridge. The other 4 markers remain in the work as guides to help line up the center of the ends when it is time to make increase rnds.

Round 6: Regular rnd. Color B.
   This rnd will be worked in the normal direction. All remaining rnds will be worked on the side that has the tail of cord and the permanent green and yellow pins.

© All Copying Prohibited By Law

1. Make bridge and turn piece around. Start with 1½ folds, skip first cord st, and work along the side toward the green end with regular Sh st. Rnd ends with 1½ folds. Connect and transfer red pin. Note: *Folds around the ends will be quite close together. Should the ends ripple a bit, do not be concerned, as the extra fullness will be taken up in later rnds.*

Round 7: Regular rnd. Color B. Repeat 6th rnd.
Round 8: Regular rnd. Color B. Repeat 6th rnd.
⁕ *Round 9*: (14 increases each end). Color A.
Increases for this rnd will be made in *every other stitch* around each end. Half the total number of inc will be made before the CT, the remaining half after the CT first inc will be made in the 14th cord st before the CT. Last inc will fall in the 13th cord st after CT.

Read *Helpful Hints: Marking center top of oval ends* before you continue.

Round 10: Regular rnd. Color B.
Round 11: Regular rnd. Color B.
Round 12: Regular rnd. Color B.
⁕*Round 13*: (16 increases each end). Color A.
Increases for this rnd will be made in *every other stitch* around each end. Follow directions for establishing CT and marking position of increase area.
Start first increase in 16th cord st to the right of CT.
Last increase will fall in 15th cord st to the left of CT.
Round 14: Final round. Color A.
Pull off 2 folds in *every other stitch* down the sides and around both ends.

Helpful Hints: How to decide length of oval center

When you have decided the size of the oval piece you wish to make, subtract the finished width you want your piece to be from the finished length you want. The difference between these two figures will be the length of the starting chain stitch row. Thus, for the 7" x 10" table mat, the difference between the finished width and length is 3", so the starting chain stitch row should be 3".

A 1' chain stitch row will make a rug 1' x 2' or 2' x 3' or 3' x 4' depending on how many rounds are made. Regardless of the finished size, there will always be approximately 12" difference between the finished width and length.

A chain stitch row that is 18" will make a rug that is 1' x 2½' or 1½' x 3' or 2' x 3½'. A 24" chain stitch row will make a rug 1' x 3', up to 9' x 11' or larger. A 6' x 9' or 7' x 10' or 9' x 12' rug would require a 36" chain stitch row.

© All Copying Prohibited By Law

How to mark center top of oval ends for increase round

To distribute increases evenly around the oval ends to keep them symmetrical, it is necessary to establish the center top (CT) of each end. Half the increasing will be done on the right side of the CT, and half will be done on the left side.

1. Use the permanent pin markers that were put in place in the first rnd, and the pins left in place after the fifth rnd, as guides. If the pins have been lost, use tail of cord to help locate the center of the first rnd.

2. Lay a ruler (or a yardstick as piece grows larger) along the starting row. Line it up evenly with the pin markers.

3. Where ruler crosses the oval ends, place a pin marker in that fold at each end. Pin outside of fold through single thickness to mark the position of the CT at each end.

4. Count cord stitches to the right of the CT and put a marker (pin or paper clip) through the cord stitch to indicate where first increase for this round will be made. Remove these markers as you work up to them.

5. Count cord stitches to the left of the CT and mark position where last increase will fall.

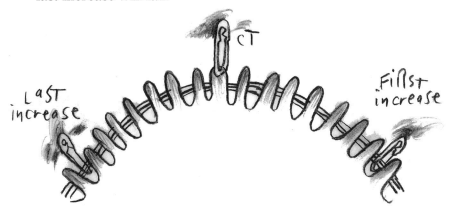

When increasing in *every other stitch* on the ends, an easy way to count as you go along is 1 and 2 and 3 and 4, etc. When you count 1, that is the first increase, "and" is a regular stitch, 2 is the second increase, etc. After completing the increase sequence, it is advisable to separate the round just completed with your fingers and check to be sure you have pulled off 2 folds after every other stitch for the total number of increases required.

© All Copying Prohibited By Law

Chapter Four

Using Shirrét

© All Copying Prohibited By Law

Now that you've completed a Shirrét, you'll want to know how to finish it properly—and how to use it and care for it for many, many years to come.

Blocking your finished work

The appearance of your work will be greatly improved with blocking. Any cupping or slight rippling can be corrected at this time.

For small pieces, wrap piece in a wet turkish towel. Leave in towel long enough for piece to absorb sufficient moisture to feel damp. Remove from wet towel. Pat to shape. Dry on flat surface. A webbed lawn chair, cake cooling rack, or sweater drying rack will allow air to circulate underneath. Piece may be put in dryer on "Air" or low heat cycle to fluff and finish drying process.

For large pieces, lay on floor or flat surface on several damp towels (large beach towels are good). Use plastic tablecloth or dry cleaner bags underneath to protect the floor or table. Cover with damp towels and leave until piece has absorbed enough moisture to feel damp. Remove from towels and lay on flat surface. Shape with hands so piece is symmetrical and flat. Turn to dry underside. May be put in dryer on "Air" or low heat to fluff and dry thoroughly.

Cleaning Shirrét

It is recommended that you spray your Shirrét when new or recently cleaned with a fabric protector, such as Scotch Guard®. With this protection they will remain fresh and clean for quite some time.

Large rugs can be cleaned with a vacuum cleaner. Use attachments or electric broom for small rugs. Shake kitchen and bathroom rugs to remove loose dust. Cotton and wool rugs can be washed, unless too large to handle easily when wet (which makes them very heavy and puts a strain on the cord). Cold water soap used with cool water is best for most fabrics. If the Shirrét is heavily soiled or stained, add an enzyme pre-soak. Soak long enough to remove all soil, then rinse several times. Don't twist or wring. Put in automatic washer on spin cycle or squeeze out water and wrap in towels to absorb remaining moisture. Shirrét may also be put in washer for short rinse cycle at slow speed, and spin cycle. Small hot mats may be included with regular laundry.

To dry, lay on towels on flat surface with plastic underneath to protect table or floor. Shape with hands to smooth out any imperfections. Turn over to dry completely. May be put in dryer on low heat to finish drying and to fluff.

The easiest method is to take all pieces, large or small, cotton or wool, to the coin dry cleaning machines. It is fast and everything comes out beautifully clean and ready for immediate use. Chair pads and small rugs can be included

© All Copying Prohibited By Law

with a load of clothing. There is no linting or raveling. But if there are any stains, check with a dry cleaning professional first so they don't get baked in.

Foam rug cleaners and carpet shampoos also produce satisfactory results.

Decorating with Shirrét

If Shirrét were a painting you would hang it on the wall. So think of it as art! Try a small round rug laid across the back of a comfy chair with pillows. On a wood floor, use rubber non-slip rug backing under your Shirrét. You can put Shirrét on top of carpeting, in front of love seats, as a hearth rug by the fireplace, beside a bed, in an entry hall or stair landing. Shirrét on a floor cushion is exotic. Yes, you can hang Shirrét on the wall, by lacing colored threads under the crochet stitches along the top edge, and looping them over a wooden dowel.

© All Copying Prohibited By Law

Can you find the Shirrét in this picture?
From left to right—
Half-round hearth rug of wool
Doll house ribbon Shirrét - four, one
    on couch back
Rainbow wall hanging "*Ecology 1*" of
    cotton
Floor pillow of patchwork squares
Cat-shaped welcome rug of wool
Shirrét slippers! wool, doubled strips
    on the sole
Room sized round of wool
Long oval bench pad of cotton
Medium oval in cotton
Shirrét thermal vest of mohair and
    light-weight wools
Round chair pads - four 'targets' in
    Caribbean colors
Tea mug-warmer in wool
Hot mat
Tea pot cozy in wool
Long rectangular bench pad

Fun with Shirrét: Community fundraiser

Shirrét is a great cooperative community project. You can begin by assembling the fabrics to reuse. Separate them into either wool or cotton. Cut the seams off old clothes.

    In a group meeting you can cut the strips. Bring steam irons, marking gauges and soap slivers. Then you can share and exchange strips, and think about the color design of your patchwork Shirrét sampler. Try to have a color theme so that the individually made squares will relate to each other. Everyone makes squares of a certain size, say 6". Save a good amount of the fabric that you use in the squares for the border.

    When the squares are done, lay out the pieces to design the overall rugs. Explore several options at this stage; don't rush to design it. Don't forget that warm reds, oranges and yellows attract the eye! You might make six patchwork rugs from the squares; or two larger rugs; or one runner and one square; or ten hotmats, one hearth rug and two chair pads. Lace the patchwork squares together and add a border that includes different fabrics from the body of the piece. They'll look good in your display because they'll all go together. You will have some valuable Shirrét for a raffle or auction!

© All Copying Prohibited By Law

Patterns

© All Copying Prohibited By Law

Rows

Candy stripe mat

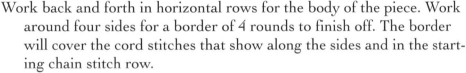

Chair pad for a child's chair or hot mat under
hot dishes

Size: 8" x 9½" with lengthwise stripes

Materials: Medium-weight woven 45" - 60" fabric
(cotton-polyester blend duck or 100% cotton). Beginners should stay away from tightly
woven percales or double knits.

1/4 yard each - Color A (Yellow), B (Pink),
C (Green), D (Lavender)

1/8 yd. each - Color E (Blue), F (Peach) or
substitutes

Mat can also be made from 1 yard of print or plaid
for the center, and coordinate 1/8 yard each of
2 solid colors for the border.

Approx. 100 yds. 4-ply cotton Shirrét Cord

5 Marking Pins

Work back and forth in horizontal rows for the body of the piece. Work
around four sides for a border of 4 rounds to finish off. The border
will cover the cord stitches that show along the sides and in the starting chain stitch row.

Fill needle with 41 full folds. Make slip loop. Follow directions previously
given for Shirrét sampler. Starting chain stitch row should have 40
chain stitches and 41 folds (which includes an extra 1/2 fold on each
end). There are 19 rows in the body of the mat in the following color
sequence: A (ch st row), B C E A F D
C B A F B D E C A B E C.

Candy stripe mat in crosswise stripes

Size: 8½" x 11½" with crosswise stripes.
This mat complements the previous
pattern, and the two are perfect for a
child's chair seat and back.

Materials: Same as 8" x 9½" Candy
Stripe mat

Procedure: Follow directions previously
given for 8" x 9½" mat. Starting chain
stitch row should have 34 ch sts and

© All Copying Prohibited By Law

folds with an extra 1/2 fold on each end. There are 32 rows in the body of the mat in the following color sequence:

A (ch st row), B, C, E, A, F, D, C, B, A, F, B, D, E, C, A, B, E, C, D, A, F, E, D, C, A, B, E, C, F, B, A.

Border: A, B, C, D.

Stripey chair pad in wool

Size: 12" x 13¹⁄₄"
Materials: Medium weight 54-60" 100% wool or wool blends
5/8 yd. lavender/blue/gold plaid (A)
1/4 yd. each: light blue (B), lavender (C)
1/8 yd. each: light green (D), camel (E)
Approximately 175 yds. 4-ply cotton Shirrét cord
Procedure: Follow directions for Candy Stripe mat, 8" x 9¹⁄₂". Starting chain stitch row (Color A) should have 54 ch sts and folds with an extra 1/2 fold on each end. There are 35 rows in the body of the piece in the following color sequence:

Rows 2,3,4: A.	Rows 5,6: B.
Rows 7,8,9: A.	Rows 10,11: D.
Rows 12, 13,14: A.	Rows 15,16: E.
Rows 17,18,19: A.	Rows 20,21: C.
Rows 22,23,24: A.	Rows 25,26: D.
Rows 27,28,29: A.	Rows 30,31: B.
Rows 32,33,34,35: A.	

Border rnd 1: Color C. Pick up 52 sts along each side and work 54 sts across each end. Pull off 4 folds in last stitch of each row to turn the corner. Pinmark to establish location.

Rnd 2: Color B. At each of the 4 pinmarked corners, increase in the first stitch, make a regular st in the next stitch, inc in the next st. Pinmark the st in between the 2 increases.

Rnd 3: Color A. **Final round**: Pull off 2 folds in *every other* stitch. At corners, on either side of pinmarked center st, pull off 4 folds. Pull off only 1 fold in center stitch.

© All Copying Prohibited By Law

See page 47, and see *Fun with Shirrét: Community fundraiser* on page 71.

Rounds

"Old Sturbridge" round 14 ¹/₂" chair pad in wool

Materials: Medium-weight 54-60" wool or wool blends

Color A (check or plaid): 1/4 yd.

Colors B, C, D, E (solid colors) 1/4 yd. each

Color pattern: Center through 9th rnd: Color A (beige, tan, green)

Rnds 10, 11: Color B (olive green)

Rnd 12: Color C (camel)

Rnds 13, 14: Color D (aqua)

Rnds 15, 16: Color E (chartreuse)

Rnd 17: Color B

Rnd 18: Color A

Rnds 19, 20: Color C

Rnd 21: Color E

Rnd 22: Color D

Rnd 23: Color D and
Color B

Center through 14th rnd: Follow pattern for 8" round table mat.

Rnds 15 - 19: regular rounds

20th rnd: Increase *in every other stitch*. Total folds at end of round should be 243.

Rnds 21 and 22: Regular rounds.

23rd rnd: *Final round*. Use 2 thicknesses - 1 strip of Color D and 1 strip of Color B, threaded on needle so Color B will be on the outside of finished piece. Be sure to begin and end all strips with cut edges turned to the inside. Pull off 1 fold (double thickness) *in every stitch*. Block finished piece.

© All Copying Prohibited By Law

Ovals

Oval chairside rug in wool, 16" x 24"

This little rug is a good size to use in front of a chair. Not only will it provide delightfully soft rug for the feet, but it will prevent worn carpet if used in front of a favorite armchair (or cover a worn spot that may already exist). Plan your color scheme to coordinate with the chair, and it will add an attractive decorator touch to the room. This is also a good size to use in a room doorway where carpet wear is often noticeable.

Materials: Medium weight woven 100% wool, or blended wool, orlon, acrylics, etc. Approx. 2 3/8 yd. 54"- 60."
Cord: approx. 300 yds. Marking Pins
Background (plaid, check, stripe)... 1¹/₂ yd.
Color A (solid color)...1/2 yd.
Color B (solid color)... 3/8 yd.

Color Pattern:
Center thru 9th Rnd: Background Fabric
Rnd 10: Color A
Rnd 11: Color B
Rnd 12: Color A
Rnds 13 thru 17: Background Fabric
Rnd 18: Color B
Rnds 19, 20: Color A
Rnds 21 thru 27: Background Fabric
Rnds 28, 29: Color A
Rnd 30: Color B

Center thru Rnd 13: Follow directions for 7 x 10" Oval table mat. Make chain stitch row 8" long. Make color changes according to color pattern above.
Rnds 14, 15,16: Regular rnds.
Rnd 17: (18 increases each end). Follow directions for marking center tops of ovals (p. 67). Mark position of increase area. Increases for this round will be made in *every third stitch.* Start first increase in 26th cord stitch before CT. Last increase will fall in 26th cord stitch after CT. The increase around each oval end will look like this:

x11x11x11x11x11x11x11x11x11 / x11x11x11x11x11x11x11x11x

Each x represents an inc stitch, with regular stitches in between. The line in the center represents the pin marker at the center top (CT) of the oval end.

© All Copying Prohibited By Law

Rnds 18, 19, 20: Regular rnds.

Rnd 21: (21 increases each end).

Increase in *every third stitch*. Start first inc in 29th cord stitch before CT. Last inc will fall in 29th cord st after CT.

Rnds 22,23,24,25: Regular rnds.

Rnd 26: (22 increases each end).

Increase in *every fourth stitch*. Start first inc in 43rd st before CT. Last inc will fall in 42nd st after CT.

Rnds 27,28 29: Regular rnds.

Rnd 30: Final round. Pull off 2 folds in *every other stitch* down the sides and around both ends. See *How to block finished work so it lays flat.*

Oval rug in cotton, 18 x 30"

This rug is designed to be made with a print fabric for the background and two color bands using three coordinated solid colors.

Materials: Medium weight woven cotton or blended fabric, approx. 6 yds. 45." Cord: approx 700 yds.

Background: 3 yds.

Color A: 1⅜ yd.

Color B: 3/8 yd.

Color C: 1¼ yd.

Color Pattern: Center through Rnd 9: Background Fabric

Rnds 10,11: Color A	Rnd 12: Color B
Rnds 13,14: Color A	Rnds 15 thru 23: Background fabric
Rnds 24,25: Color A	Rnd 26: Color C
Rnd 27: Color B	Rnd 28: Color C
Rnds 29, 30: Color A	Rnds 31 thru 36: Background Fabric
Rnds 37, 38: Color C	

Center thru 21st rnd: Follow Pattern: 16"x 24" chairside rug. Make chain stitch row 12" long, and color changes according to color pattern above.

Rnds 22,23,24: regular rnds.

25th Rnd: (22 increases each end).

Increase in *every 4th stitch*. Start first inc in 43rd st before CT. Last inc will fall in 42nd stitch after CT .

Rnds 26,27,28,29: regular rnds.

© All Copying Prohibited By Law

*30th Rnd: (24 increases each end).

Increase in *every 4th stitch*. Start first inc in 47th stitch before CT. Last inc will fall in 46th stitch after CT.

Rnds 31,32,33,34: regular rnds.

*35th Rnd: (26 increases each end).

Increase in *every 5th stitch*. Start first inc in 63rd stitch before CT. Last inc will fall in the 63rd stitch after CT.

Rnds 36 and 37: Regular rnds.

Rnd 38: Final round. pull off 2 folds in *every other stitch* down the sides and around both ends. See *How to block finished piece*.

Follow this same increase progression for larger rugs. Wool, because of its heavier weight and body, requires fewer rounds to attain a given size. Also, you may have to make changes in the placement of increase rounds.

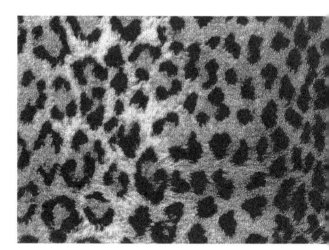

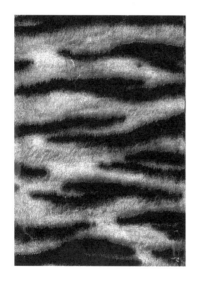

© All Copying Prohibited By Law

Making Your Own Patterns

When making a piece that must exactly fit a given area—for example, a chair or bench seat, stair treads or a rug that is to be used in a particular place—it is very helpful to first cut a paper pattern. Use newspaper or plain wrapping paper.

For a round chair pad, measure the size of the chair seat. With a compass or string and pencil, draw a circle on paper and cut it out. Place it on the chair seat to be sure the size is correct. A 14" or 14½" diameter circle is a good size for most medium chairs. For larger seats a 15½" or larger chair pad may be required. In cotton, make the chair pad slightly smaller than the actual size of the seat because the cotton will spread a bit with use.

For a square chair pad it is advisable to make the body of the piece somewhat smaller than you think you need because you can always add another round of border to bring the chair pad up to size if necessary.

For an oval pattern, fold the rectangle in fourths. Mark off half of the desired finished width and length. Connect the two points in an oval curve and cut on this line.

When you have the proper size pattern in paper, use it as a guide against which to measure your piece as you work. Lay your work on the pattern as you progress, so you can measure and determine color changes. It is also helpful to try your color plan in advance. Lay fabric strips on your paper pattern, or sketch with markers, to try out your color placement.

How to make a gauge to determine the size your rugs will be.

When you follow a pattern, or when you make your own pattern, you need to have a gauge to know the size your rugs will be.

You can make a gauge by assuming that in medium-bodied cotton, five folds of Shirrét are 1" wide and that four rows are 1" high. In medium-weight wool, 4½ folds are 1" wide and four rows are 1½" high.

Cotton:
5 folds = 1" wide
4 rows = 1" high

Wool:
4½ folds = 1" wide
4 rows = 1½" high

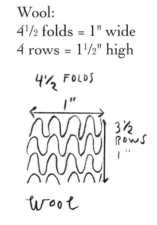

Cotton

Wool

© All Copying Prohibited By Law

The bulk of the fabric you use, the size of the folds you make as you fill the needle, and the tension of your crochet stitches all determine your gauge, *which may be different from this average*, so please measure your sample to make your own gauge.

Planning a design

There are unlimited possiblities for the use of designs in Shirrét, from folk art and ethnic motifs to pictorials. Because of the linear characteristic of the shirred folds, designs based on horizontal and vertical lines are worked in squares or rectangles that are done in rows. Curves and arcs work best in round or oval Shirrét.

Simplicity of design is more effective than complex detail. Native American designs lend themselves beautifully to Shirrét, especially Navajo designs with their repetition of geometric shapes: blocks, crosses, zigzags, triangles and diamonds. Oriental rug designs also provide many motifs that can be adapted effectively.

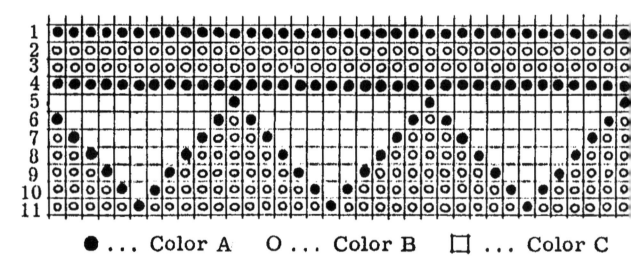

● ... Color A   O ... Color B   □ ... Color C

Geometric motif

This constant repeat pattern can be modified and used in many ways. Each motif has 12 stitches, so the pattern requires a multiple of 12 in order to come out even.

© All Copying Prohibited By Law

To apply this design to the 14¹/₂" Chair Pad in Cotton: use rows 4 through 11 of the graph.

On **Rnd 19**: eliminate 3 of the increases, so the total folds at the end of the rnd will be 240 (a multiple of 12).

Rnd 20: Color A.

Rnd 21: Fill needle with 11 folds of Color C and 1 fold of Color A, alternating. Start rnd with 1¹/₂ folds of A. Skip first cord st as usual. Rnd ends with 11¹/₂ folds of C.

Rnd 22: Turn piece over and work in reverse direction. Fill needle by reading graph in reverse (from left to right). Rnd starts with 1¹/₂ A, ends with 1¹/₂ B.

Rnd 23: Normal direction. Rnd starts 2¹/₂ B. Ends 1¹/₂ B.

Rnd 24: Reverse direction. Start with 2¹/₂ B. End with 3¹/₂ B.

Rnd 25: Normal direction. Rnd starts with 4¹/₂ B, end 5¹/₂ B.

Rnd 27: Normal. Start 6¹/₂ B, end 5¹/₂ B.

On round and oval pieces, design motifs will line up more accurately if the work is turned around and worked in reverse direction on every other round of the design section. Follow same procedure for reversing direction as was used in the center of an oval, Rnds 3 and 5.

Designs from Graphed Patterns

Designs graphed for needlepoint, knitting and cross stitch embroidery are readily available in books and magazines and can be adapted for use in Shirrét. Graphed patterns are based on the proportions of a square because needlepoint and cross stitches are square. Each box of the graph represents a stitch that is as tall as it is wide. However, Shirrét stitches are not square; they are taller than they are wide. If you followed a graphed pattern using one Shirrét stitch per each square, your Shirrét would be elongated instead of reproducing the pattern.

For most Shirréters, two Shirrét stitches make a square equal to one square in the graph. Compare your stitches to this gauge. If you make tinier folds when you fill the needle, if your cord stitches are tighter, and if you use thin fabric, you may have three stitches to the square.

Example: You wish to follow a graphed pattern for needlepoint that is 60 squares wide. The pattern of the first row has 10 black stitches alternating with 10 white stitches across the row. With two Shirrét stitches per square, there are 20 black folds alternating with 20 white folds. At the end of the row you will have 120 folds (plus 1/2 fold on each end) instead of the 60 stitches on the pattern. The Shirrét should be a rather accurate adaptation of the design.

© All Copying Prohibited By Law

Increasing in graphed designs

When including designs in round and oval pieces, it is necessary to consider the requirements of the increasing to keep the piece flat.

The easiest approach is to plan a design that can be completed between increase rounds. If it's necessary to increase while working in pattern, do not follow the regular increase sequence that applies at that point. Instead, try to make all the increases in the background areas of the design, or in certain places in the design motifs. Increase in a uniform manner to maintain the symmetry of the design, even if you increase a little more or a little less than the normal sequence.

Glossary *of terms and abbreviations*

Bridge. The two chain stitches of cord that carry you up to the level of the new row or round.

Center Top (CT). The halfway point in the center of the oval end in an oval piece.

Cord. The 4-ply cotton thread used for the crochet stitches.

Cord Over Hook. Twist hook around cord to form a loop on the hook.

Cord Stitch. The two strands of cord between shirred folds.

Fold. A shirred fold. A double thickness of fabric makes one complete fold.

Half Fold. Half of a shirred fold. A single thickness of fabric with a cut end is one half fold.

Increase (inc). Adding extra fullness to a piece by pulling off two folds instead of 1 after a crochet stitch.

Increase Round (inc rnd). Marked ✳ to indicate that extra folds will be added

Inside of Strip. Facing toward the center of the piece. On the needle, the fabric facing you on the front or top of the needle will turn over when the fold is pulled onto the piece.

Outside of Strip. Facing to the outer edge of the piece. On the needle, the fabric that faces

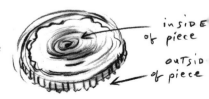

inside of piece

outsid of piece

© All Copying Prohibited By Law

down or on the back or away from you will turn over and face toward the outer edge, or outside of the piece.

Regular Round (reg rnd). One fold is pulled off for each double crochet stitch taken.

Round (rnd). One time around in a round or oval piece, working from right to left from the center out. The beginning and end are connected to form a complete unit. A connected round or oval is not a spiral. It is a full circle.

Row. A horizontal row in a square or rectangular piece, working across *from right to left*.

Shirrét Stitch (Sh st). A crochet stitch of cord *plus* a shirred fold (or folds, when increasing) of fabric from the needle.

Shirring. Running the Shirrét needle in and out through a strip of fabric to form shirred folds.

Slip Stitch (sl st). Insert hook in a stitch, cord over hook. With a single motion, draw loop through stitch and on through loop on hook.

Square Knot. The cord is usually continuous from the beginning to the end of a piece. But if you have to cut it or add new cord, secure it with a square knot. Lay right strand over left strand and twist around once, as if tying a shoelace. Then lay left end over right end and twist around once. Pull to tighten knot. Ends may be trimmed close to knot, which will work invisibly into a stitch.

© All Copying Prohibited By Law

Index

© All Copying Prohibited By Law